Y.O.U.
&
THE ULTIMATE LIFE TOOL®

FOR A BETTER MANKIND®

Y.O.U.
&
The Ultimate Life Tool®

"Cutting Edge Nature-Based Human Assessment
Technology for a Better Mankind"

Dr. Zannah Hackett

authorHOUSE®

FIRST EDITION

Library of Congress Control Number:
Hackett, Zannah
Y.O.U. & The Ultimate Life Tool®

ISBN: 978-1-4490-4735-1 (sc)
ISBN: 978-1-4490-4736-8 (hc)
ISBN: 978-1-4490-4737-5 (e)
Library of Congress Control Number: 2010900760
AuthorHouse™
1663 Liberty Drive
Bloomington, IN 47403
www.authorhouse.com
Phone: 1-800-839-8640
©2010 Dr. Zannah Hackett. All rights reserved.
First published by AuthorHouse 4/8/2010

Publisher's Note:
This book is not intended to provide personalized legal, accounting, financial, investment, or psychological advice. Readers are encouraged to seek the counsel of competent professionals to address matters of personal conflict, growth, and personal financial planning. The Author and Publisher specifically disclaim any liability, loss, or risk which is incurred as a consequence, directly or indirectly, of the use and application of any of the contents of this work.

Printed in the United States
Set in Arial
Designed by DH Design

DEDICATION

This book is dedicated to those who no longer desire to know who they are but rather prefer to know what they are, why they are here, and how they can help to make this brief life experience enjoyable for everyone.

Contents

FOREWORD

I am special. This is not meant to sound vain or boastful; however, I now know that everyone is special and I am a part of the everyone equation. The unfortunate oversight in today's world is that few realize their uniqueness, since most gauge themselves on what others think. Many have even gone so far as to organize their lives based on what others want. As an example, young children are often guided by their parents to grow up in Mom or Dad's footsteps. They are encouraged or often pushed to step into a predetermined career or business, whether it be the classical medical doctor or attorney or the construction worker or author. Once these individuals mature, they often assess their success on what others think is normal or optimum. If your friends like to be the center of attention and you do not, you are likely to be labeled *shy* or *a loner.* If your friends like camping and backpacking and you do not, you may be described as a *snob* or worse yet, *no fun.* Conversely, if a young girl did not play with dolls, she was called a *tomboy.* I do not know if I always knew I was special, but I do know now. The Knowledge of Y.O.U. has confirmed for me that what I am, in my specialness, is good, okay, and absolutely perfect for me.

Growing up, I always had an affinity for nature and a desire to be with animals. I would wander the hills in Belmont, California as a child, reaching out to what felt real and truthful in the plants and creatures surrounding me. I would venture off by myself to go sliding down grassy knolls while sitting on a cardboard box. When my parents would take the family camping in Big Sur, I found pleasure in silently swimming alone in the streams while marveling at nature, just happy to watch the leaves float past me. I delighted in these adventures and looked forward to the solitude. I was quiet and labeled shy by some and a tomboy by others. When I was given these labels and called these names, it felt like I was doing something wrong. It left me with the impression that I was different and not approved of by others, since I was not like them.

I did well being alone and quiet, and perhaps that is the reason I blend well with nature and animals. For me, it is easier to feel their presence, and I sense that they feel safe in my presence where there is no talking. Years later, an education in biochemistry at the University of California at Berkeley led to a technical position at the University of California at San Diego in reproductive medicine, which in turn led to a thirty-plus-year career studying reproductive endocrinology in wild animals at the Zoological Society of San Diego. Funny how all of that works; I was once again studying and observing animals. Instead of sitting in the hills of Belmont, California, I now found myself sitting in the mountains of Rwanda with groups of mountain gorillas and staring forest buffalo eye to eye, or in the mountains of China, sitting with the giant panda, and in Sri Lanka with elephants, and so much more. My career was based on the development of laboratory techniques to monitor the animals' reproductive status and the reaction to stressors. This was done both in the zoo setting and in their natural setting in the wild. These studies demanded my "think outside the box" creativity, my organizational and leadership qualities to bring the right people together for collaborative studies, and my ability to be alone and to be quiet. Many of these things for which I was criticized as a child were now critical to my success as a scientist.

I met Zannah Hackett in 2004. I was looking for the best love relationship for me, and a friend suggested I go to Zannah's seminar to learn how to recognize the best kind of man for me. I almost did not go, but I am very glad I did. This was a seminar filled with women. I sat on the sidelines, watching and listening. What Zannah shared seemed so simple: to assess oneself and others by this well-thought-out methodology. I liked what I heard and called her later for a personal appointment. One thing led to another, and I suggested that the information Zannah was teaching be made into an online assessment, so more people could take advantage of it. She agreed. Now that this has been accomplished, anyone can find out how special they are. As a co-founder of this company, I have now reviewed thousands of assessment results. I have found that no one is exactly like me. I am special. Everyone else is special too. I have not calculated the statistics, but the odds of finding two alike are simply too high for words. I enjoy sharing these findings with others and comparing slightly different survey results to each other, in order to see how slight differences affect the whole. The science of this knowledge is growing, and it is fascinating.

This knowledge is a wonderful body of information. It has the potential of bringing peace to relationships, to families, to the classroom, to the workplace, to corporations, and to the world by simply teaching and showing people how special they are. We can see that each of us is perfect and do what we innately do, because that is what we are. I am quiet because I have a natural characteristic uniquely personal to me that requires me to have time to myself. I require aloneness to refuel myself. I marvel at the uniqueness and sparkle of nature because another quality in me offers a childlike perspective of the world. I bring order to scientific studies because I am required to bring order to my space. I blend well with others, including animals and nature, because of these characteristics. The aspects of this knowledge go far beyond what we are currently teaching. We are discovering new intricacies through quantifying this knowledge each day as we monitor more and more people. The potential here is immense: to bring goodwill to people through the simple knowledge of discovering what we are and knowing that each of us is special in our own uniqueness. Through that uniqueness, we can work and love together … think Nobel Peace Prize here … the possibility is huge!

Nanz Zekela
YCG Co-Founder & Scientist
Papoose Conservation Wildlife Foundation
www.papoosewildlife.org

ACKNOWLEDGMENTS

I can't imagine this book ever coming to fruition without the commitment and devotion of several very important people in my life. When I first began to share the knowledge with others, it seemed as if all the right people started to show up.

In my 2004 knowledge debut, after seven years of research, I rented a space at a local center, and thirty lovely ladies graced me with their presence. I had no book, no polished PowerPoint presentation to wow them with, just me and a head full of information. My husband had lovingly designed a couple of poster graphics that I had mounted to foam core for the purposes of offering visual input, and I had no expectations of what the audience response might be. I was still very unsure of how the subject matter would be received but felt compelled to share. I am a firm subscriber to the thought, "You won't know until you try," and given this, I took a deep breath and began to convey my findings. This was a different kind of audience. Prior to this, I spent years sitting in think tanks and exploring human nature through educational coursework, living experiments, travel, and serendipitous acquaintances, all of which truly have served as a golden link in my chain of good. It was clear that everything I had to say could very well go right over their heads. In the audience were women ranging in age from twenty-five to seventy, all wondering how to create magnetic relationships in their lives. Some were single, some married, and some just struggling with relationships at work. The premise was "love"—how to go about knowing what and who is right for you, and how to nurture it once you have it. The information supporting my strategy around this pursuit was very different from any of the sage old self-help-inspired guru information on the market. Instead, it was somewhat scientific and spoke little of the dynamics of a relationship but instead addressed why the dynamics existed at all. The presentation lasted three hours. Several asked questions, some laughed, and one lady in particular sat quietly to my right like an angel in the room. She later came up to me, intrigued by my work and needing to know more. She saw the significance and the challenges with re-introducing a silent language into the world, realizing that man had unknowingly buried it in his own vain imaginings.

The curious woman that approached me that evening was Nanz Zekela. Today she is my wonderful business partner and has helped to translate and develop this technologically. Both she and I realized in doing this that others might re-acquaint themselves with a more natural perspective of reality. This would lead to a better understanding of human nature and human potential. Nanz Zekela, former scientist for thirty years with the San Diego Zoo, saw the connection. As a graduate of UC Berkeley, Nanz specialized in reproductive endocrinology, which led to extensively studying animal biology in nature. In addition, she participated as a key expert in the advancement of raising pandas in captivity for the preservation of the species. Her years of research and experience have taken her to China, Africa, and various other parts of our world where nature still exists untouched. She was and always will be a treasure to this experience.

My husband, David Hackett, curiously stood in the wings for several years prior to my first seminar and when Nanz came on the scene, he began observing and listening. Shortly thereafter, I requested his help in designing graphics for curricula; he stepped up to the plate and then some. Later, along with Hal Taylor, our current board president, he went through the certification program. Having helped many young men in recovery, David found this knowledge to be beyond Alcoholics Anonymous and offered those with time in sobriety an opportunity to add self-perception to their tool kit. He also found it key in providing an alternative to AA for those that were not drawn to the AA way of life. This was the beginning of a powerful male representation of the Knowledge of Y.O.U.. "DH" and "the Halinator" have been informative, inspirational, and entertaining in delivering talks to executives in transition. In fact, many amazing individuals have committed themselves to this work, and several stories are provided in chapter 13 entitled "Intelligence Reports." They, along with dynamic professionals like Dr. Charles Richards, Nick Pearce, Niloo Tavangar, Angie Swartz, Arlene Clements, Lisa Lehr, Kimberly Alkema, Kerri Gobbo, Danielle Fuhrman, Carol Lang, Kelli Adame, Karen Scanlon, Jill Lackey, Sheri Harvey, Denise Scahill, Mark Bishop, Martha Blanco, Rochelle Monroe, Ameya Bela and others set a standard of excellence that continues to influence the pathway of promise that lies ahead for this technology. However, when it came to writing this book, I was overwhelmed by the thought. With writing curriculum, training trainers, creating deliverables for various industries, filing for accreditations, and policing the integrity of the technology, I simply became breathless at the thought of having to spend another brain cell on anything. Then came "Praks to the rescue." Praks is a term we use to describe YCG certified practitioners. Lisa Nelson, Dr. Beth Wade, and Christine Hughes convinced me that a writers' retreat was in order. In less than a week, the four of us were seated around a large table with laptops humming. I had already completed a few chapters, and the book was completely outlined, as I had gone through the motions of putting a formal proposal together. Lisa and Dr. Beth were well trained, and I could trust them to address a case scenario and elaborate upon a concept without varying from the truth of the matter.

Lisa Nelson has been by my side every step of the way since 2006. She has embraced every new concept, new deliverable, new strategy, and new finding. When she first came to me, she was an etiquette coach—poised, elegant, and humble. Diplomacy and innocence became her like an expensive fragrance, and thanks to the knowledge, I was quick to realize that her gifts were many. She continues to lead the way as YCG's next generation of incredible experts in this technology. Being somewhat older myself, tomorrow's leaders are very important to me, as this technology is positioned to open the eyes of mankind. It can change the way we see reality and manifest unconditional love beyond that of a healthy parental relationship.

Like Lisa, God has blessed me with many incredible messengers, all on task and dedicated to carrying out their purpose in this lifetime. Christine Hughes was among them. She came to my door one day, seeking clarity, willing and ready to see the beautiful perfection of herself. Standing there, a divine soul ahead of her time, I could sense her frustration and loneliness, living in a world that moves far too slowly for her natural pace. Today, with her many gifts and outstanding talent for making miracles, she spends her time making dreams come true. Her motto, "for a better mankind," serves as the heartbeat of her daily pursuits. As a YCG certified practitioner, she is passionate and driven to make sure as many people as can be reached are privy to this knowledge and technology. She knows it is the missing piece in psychometrics and psychology today. I know she understands that *peace* on Earth is a pipe dream until everyone can *see* each other, either in person or otherwise. She believes that we are the *hope* for the future. Knowing that her vision for tomorrow is embedded in the spirit of who she is, I am confident that her contribution to this lifetime exceeds all expectations. Her brilliant mind for finance while managing the challenges of life and career sets a new standard of excellence, and YCG is forever grateful for her commitment and dedication. We would not be where we are in this moment without her.

Shortly after meeting Christine, I met Dr. Beth at the Mayor's Breakfast in Encinitas, California. We sat next to each other, started talking, and have never stopped. I realized what a wonderful, natural, healing disposition she had and knew instantly that she would be a great team member. She and I are the same age and come from similar backgrounds; it was comforting to have a friend and colleague who was in the same space and time as myself. Being a mother of sons as well, we shared the woes and wonders of motherhood and how fortunate we were to have been blessed in this way. Women with sons seem to viscerally understand the imbalance between men and women today. Beth brings laughter and wisdom born out of having survived the heartaches and victories of life. Her love for leaving a legacy of having lived a purposeful life rings loud and clear with every presentation that pours from her heart in sharing the knowledge. Having founded the Genesis Center, and specializing in energy medicine, she has made a notable difference in helping children with autism, as well as individuals seeking personal healing. When I asked Beth to help me chronicle case studies for the book, she immediately volunteered. Her literary contribution to this book has been substantial, and were it not for the collaborative efforts of all who believe in my work, this book would not be available today.

It is with a warm heart and tears in my eyes that I joyfully report that this work is here to stay. Thanks to the many YCG certified practitioners who cared enough to change lives for the better every day. You are the angels assigned to lift the veil of subjective understanding so that others may *see* and embrace the authenticity of this lifetime. I love you.

INTRODUCTION

"Who am I?" is a question that has intrigued and plagued mankind since the beginning of time. Regardless of our gender, race, creed, political ideology, or social standing, each of us longs to know and love ourselves deeply and unconditionally. In truly knowing ourselves, we discover our purpose, and our lives hold greater meaning. The payoff is a happier, purpose-filled life, during which we can better experience the contentment and joy we should find in living. Whether this quest begins in our teens, later in life, or somewhere in between, most of us search for a deeper understanding of self at one point or another. This thirst for "inner knowledge" has led people to try everything, from mind-altering drugs to embracing a religious doctrine, in an attempt to peel themselves down to the core of their very essence. But even after all of that, there often remains a pestering voice demanding to appease the thirst to know more.

Is it even possible to "know oneself"? Is someone or something in the universe playing games with our heads? There exists within each of us a call, a whisper, and a yearning for the formula that explains our very being; it provides a reason, an excuse, and even an alibi for our wanting something different from that of another. Great numbers of people, regardless of their daily practices, will stand up and say *yes* to the opportunity to know oneself at a core level. In this work, it is revealed what motivates man and what we need to honor and feed within our self to have what we want in life. *The Knowledge of Y.O.U.®* is the result of unraveling a spun truth tangled over thousands of years. It exposes man's feeble attempt to outwit himself and his peers by overlooking the obvious. Understanding lies as much in the visible as in the invisible, and it is older than the language of man. We can find our own unique "operating manual"—information that resides inside, outside, and all around each of us—if we revisit a time that did not require words, a time when common sense was all that one required to survive. This understanding, formerly available to the naked eye, has been upstaged by the need to reason, using that which lies not in this world but instead in that which exists behind the scenes, or for some, in eternity. What has happened is that in our attempt to understand both worlds, the physical and the spiritual, many have gotten trapped in between the two understandings. With *The Knowledge of Y.O.U.®,* we are addressing the physical, recognizing that there is a reason for showing up in nature the way we do, and realizing that it holds significance in prevailing behaviors and dispositions. Acknowledging the physical is like turning the light on in a once-darkened room. Many today are searching for answers in the dark, when all they simply need to do is turn the light on (get the information that is already physically available at their fingertips) and look at what stands before them with an intelligent awareness of what one's physicality means.

Over the past four years, I have trained many professionals in the Knowledge of Y.O.U.®, each wanting to refine his or her ability to effectively communicate how simple life can truly be. This work provides comprehensive and all-inclusive "answers" to achieve measurable results in this physical world. Until now, many redundant theories, subjective methodologies, and personal belief systems have been held responsible for one's success or failure in reaching his or her potential. In contrast, this knowledge is objective, and the technology serves to enhance human understanding by quantifying the value of one's natural talents and capabilities as revealed by physical law rather than popular psychological opinion.

The Knowledge of Y.O.U.® demonstrates how science and physical law support our performance and our behavior in tandem with the natural mathematics of man or quantum physics. This knowledge originates from a time when humans had only to rely on themselves and the relationships inside and outside of themselves. This primordial insight provides answers to the questions we ask ourselves today—the very same questions posed by primitive man: How do I assess my needs for survival? How do I protect myself? How do I communicate effectively with everyone in my life? The answer to all of these questions is, "I manage to survive by gaining an understanding of what and who I am, and this lies in the obvious." The "obvious" is something that has been lost over hundreds of thousands of years. Primitive man was very proficient at enlisting the laws of nature, so much so that it afforded him the ability to survive for millions of years! Today, man often walks outside the laws of nature; never realizing how easy life could be if only he could *see.*

Where other popular theories focus on manifesting from the inside out, The Knowledge of Y.O.U.® teaches us *how to see* from the outside in and what makes us tick, thus allowing us to view others from a purely objective perspective, which ultimately dispels the judgment and disappointment in everyday life. This book is an extension of knowledge that provides the "real" answers that people are hoping to find. When we understand our self, we understand what our "maximum attractions" are, our "like attractions," and our "repulsions." We can stop wasting energy on relationships and people who are incapable of helping us achieve our goals, if we choose to. This knowledge not only changes the way we interact with others, but it impacts our expectations of ourselves and everyone around us. The magnitude of grand results is immeasurable because we no longer make decisions blindly.

Much of man's unhappiness stems from having been exposed to high levels of toxicity. This breeds opportunistic, excessive, and competitive behaviors, versus the realization that there is enough for everyone to survive in alignment with their nature.

Contrary to materialism, authentic spiritual traditions inform us that there are levels of deeper personal understanding. These can be found in the recent works of Florence Scovel Shinn, and she likely borrowed them from Emmet Fox, who, like Florence was a truth seeker. He was probably taught by another, who derived the understanding from another, and so on and so on. We can go back hundreds, even thousands of years and see that wisdom, in its many renditions, stands the test of time. In truth, there is nothing new on this planet. However, the wisdom that has prevailed holds parts of a universal equation, the silent mathematical formula that man innately understood before he could speak. The problem lies in not being able to remember this formula or even recognize it when it stands before you. In many ways, we have become blind in relying on opinion versus accessing a natural visual understanding of what we can see with our naked eye.

Human misunderstandings are further exacerbated by the fact that we continue to address the nature of man in part, rather than as a whole. This creates a misconception of providing accurate treatments for the *nature* of what ails man. Professionals specializing in psychology and human assessment still frequently prefer to use methods that treat a symptom with approved rhetoric, subjective quantified opinion, or distracting methods designed to disconnect an individual from the reality of their situation, when in fact, a full multidimensional diagnostic is in order. We must first know *what* we are working on; realizing the *who* is secondary. When we can address this problem, situations appearing as an identity crisis, insecurity, conflict, and lack of purpose will cease to exist.

Chapter One

Getting to Know Y.O.U.

Man's desire to know himself and how seeing the authenticity of all that exists in and around you will change your life forever, dismissing opinion and judgment and consciously accepting what is.

When you look at a cactus, do you anticipate shade? When you see a pine tree, do you assume it will grow in the desert? When you look at a lion, do you expect it to meow? When you glance at strangers, what do you know about them? Are they passive? Are they active? Do they see the cup half empty? Do they like order or prefer a more disheveled existence? In getting to know others, do your clients need to be touched or prefer you stay at a distance when communicating with them? Does your child need to move in order to hear you? What if you could answer all of these questions just by looking at someone? Primordial wisdom in tandem with understanding the physical science of who we are reveals all of these answers and more, without ever having to speak. It puts stillness first, sight second, and sound third. It's a three-dimensional world. Stop, look, and listen, three simple steps for accessing Y.O.U., a once-silent language of self-discovery. This same understanding literally gave primitive man a huge advantage in terms of survival. In fact, he was so poised for success that he could recognize friend or foe upon sight. His astute connectedness to intelligence, in conjunction with the laws of nature, gave us the promise of tomorrow as a species. Unfortunately, we as a species can no longer recognize itself anymore; instead we grasp for man-made solutions to natural problems. We continuously impose our own expectations upon others, insisting that what works for one will work for the other, or better yet, subscribe to popular opinion. In a sense, we have become homogenized, condensed, dumbed down, and reduced to trying to appear intelligent in an ever-evolving ignorant world. However, it doesn't have to be that way. Getting to know Y.O.U. can change one's soul search into a self-find, resulting in self-acceptance and the ability to co-exist with various types of unique individuals who see and experience life from a completely different perspective, without judgment. Ask yourself, "Does a Cadillac Escalade require more gas and accommodate more passengers than a Honda Civic?" Now ask yourself, if the Civic and the Escalade were human, "Would they likely take each other's advice when it came to fuel efficiency, tire size, and relationship management?" Would you recommend the Civic get a trailer hitch so it could haul a thirty-foot sailboat? It's absolutely unbelievable the advice we give to one another based on what works for us and a majority of others like us. We each are as unique as our fingerprint. In fact, no two leaves in nature are alike. Understanding human nature like an arborist understands trees or an auto aficionado understands cars marks the beginning of self-mastery. Getting back to nature, revisiting man's original mode of operation, affords us the ability to communicate how one can survive naturally, thus, allowing for optimum performance and reassurance of one's purpose in life.

Just imagine primitive man standing vigil with the thick forest at his back. Poised at the water's edge, he gazes upon the vast lake before him, hypnotized by the rhythm of the waves as they break in their ebb and flow upon the shore. There is no spoken language to express his awe. The birds sing in harmony with Mother Nature's song, and the gentle breezes caress his skin. His body responds instinctively to all that nature provides in silent conversation. He listens for the subtle changes in the sounds of nature to alert him to that which may help or harm his plight of survival. In an instant, he hears the rustle of the trees and reacts to its pronounced voice. The hairs stand up on his arm, and before he can blink his eyes, intelligence urges him to flee for shelter. This silent wisdom is the same intelligence that afforded him the ability to survive for hundreds of thousands of years without a language, without a cell phone, an automobile, or a million-dollar insurance policy.

For centuries, man has written about the origin of language. In 1882, an article addressing comparative philology, published by J. A. Smith, D.D., an editor of one of Chicago's leading publications, *The Standard,* reveals some interesting findings. Simply put, it states that philology (the love of language) can be traced back to a time of primitive communication, when man was able to thrive without it. In fact, the *language of love* versus the *love of language* likely prevailed. Of course, it did not have the same look and feel that love and language have today. It was more pure and honest and addressed all that man needed from nature. He was not nearly as influenced by his peers as he was by his physical surroundings and the unpredictable elements of nature. His focus was primarily directed toward staying warm, fed, and alive. His intelligence was most pronounced when addressing the obvious, versus trying to outwit another human vying for his possessions. Like wolves, there existed a mutual respect for survival, and like the wolf, man spent his energy wisely. Intelligence is not born of language, but rather intelligence gave birth to language. Maintaining the integrity of this intelligence as we speak is where self-discovery becomes of the utmost importance and where the greatest test of man plays itself out daily, hourly, and by the second. We still are striving to recognize ourselves in our own individual states of authenticity, knowing deep down inside that there is a reason why we show up the way we do in this life.

The study of the origins of language, as described in J.A. Smith's article, entitled the "Outlines of Primitive Belief," demonstrates that mankind's primitive speech was of a rudimentary character, filled with abstract sounds, unfit to express any kind of sophisticated thought. The greatest revelation in the study is that words were originally by-products of sensation and observation, not thought. This means that man's intellectual center has become more pronounced over time, much like cars having more sophisticated engines today than those of the early 1900s. Primitive man (like an infant) was in a constant state of discovery, aware of even the tiniest changes in and around him. His astute response to sound and visceral occurrences was far more pronounced than it is in man today. Man today has become desensitized as a result of being over-stimulated, and survives often by means of ignorance versus intelligence. He cares little about knowing the subtle differences between these two modes of operation, as long as desired results are produced. A simple illustration would be if someone was experiencing hunger and chose to eat potato chips instead of a baked potato to appease his appetite. Immediately the hunger is appeased, but with these kinds of non-nutritional habitual choices, toxicity builds and eventually compromises his lifespan, his performance, and the way in which it affects all that touches his life. Intelligence versus ignorance is about choice, and it can change the direction of man in an instant.

Research studies providing citations have reported that primitive man lacked intelligence, but the curious believe otherwise, realizing that intelligence had a much clearer channel. He was free from the life interruptions that we are faced with today. The noise, chatter, and incessant environmental disturbances that permeate our existence, even while we sleep, posed no threat to primitive man's access to himself or his talents. Thus, instinctive intelligence was largely responsible for man's survival and remained in charge during man's early attempt to connect with his surroundings through sound. It was not until ignorance began to infiltrate and pollute man's thought processes that intelligence began to waiver. These thought processes originally revealed themselves as physical behaviors, and these behaviors eventually became fueled by toxic outside influences. Unfortunately, the cause of many of these influences originated with man discovering how words can manipulate, intimidate, and offer a shortcut to success, rather than an intelligent route to personal freedom and self-mastery. In brief, words got us into this and only words can get us out; thus the great desire to chronicle, research, and identify the nature of intelligence. It is in the nature of all things that a formula is revealed. It is in understanding the nature of *you* that one becomes truly "on purpose" and beneficial in this lifetime. To survive a lifetime self-realized is to be free. Consequently, psychologists and relationship experts continue to try to put puzzle pieces together in an effort to get a clearer picture for their clients trapped by their own vain imaginings and misconceptions of the nature of their existence. The answer, the mathematics of our physical existence, and the key to your own understanding lies in the obvious. It shows up by "judging a book by its cover," by realizing that appearances tell a story and understanding that they are, in fact, revealing versus deceiving. All we need to know to understand everything that physically and not-so-physically exists (e.g. oxygen, the days of the week, etc.), begins by understanding what we can *see* with our eyes. Processing a visual experience naturally simply doesn't exist anymore. Man has lost access to the silent language of survival that afforded him the ability to know what was good for him and what wasn't. In this book, one will begin to *see* how nature shows up in him or her. They will begin to understand why they do what they do and how gravity, electromagnetism, nuclear forces, and the interface of these laws uniquely creates a personal roadmap to happiness.

Survival is more than getting through the day. It's about maintaining resilience and an attitude of elasticity that permits us to benefit from the laws that govern our physical existence. This ebb and flow of survival is what we refer to as the natural order of this lifetime and must be carefully monitored. Operating in the world out of ignorance (an imbalance) can bring about the demise of the species. The fall of the Roman Empire serves as a less severe example of ignorance prevailing over intelligence. In the case of the fall of Rome, language fed ignorance efficiently in bringing about the demise of this once well-intended intelligent public.

In the beginning, prehistoric man often illustrated to communicate and chronicle the significance of his experience. He would take a stick and draw in the sand or a sharp rock and carve on a wall. Petroglyphs and hieroglyphs can be found throughout the world, testifying to man's need for leaving some expression of self-significance behind. When man began to first coin terms for what he saw, his diction improved, and once he began to draw pictures to further explain his intent, he became even more audible, thus appearing progressively more intelligent. In today's world, this would look similar to a football coach communicating his strategy to his team, or a speaker providing a PowerPoint presentation.

In the previous article referenced earlier, J.A. Smith described man's first words as *"horse"," tree"," run", "river", "wolf"*, etc. He identified these as outward ideas. Assuming this theory to be accurate, it would stand to reason that man in his primitive state used language not only for survival but for impressing others as well. It was not until later, when the *physical* need of language met with the *metaphysical* need, that man gained an opportunity to advance his nature by means of using this co-creative state for purposes of good or evil. In nature, there exists a set of laws that must be adhered to, and if we choose not to abide by these laws, we—as well as every other living thing—will cease to exist. These laws (physical and metaphysical) are discussed in chapters two and three, and for purposes of describing primitive man's co-creative abilities, it is important to know that all laws intersect with one another to create form. There exists a recipe for survival and for advancement of the species that includes a gentle mixing of these laws that often produces an evolutionary by-product. This could be a hut, a new tool, the discovery of a cure for a disease, or the invention of fire. It is in the intelligent understanding of these laws that we see where *the secret or seemingly hidden truth* lives. However, it is in referencing intelligence as a "secret," that demonstrates man's ignorance, which often stirs up arguments and creates disease. When we can recognize ignorance we elicit creativity. Instead of vain imaginings, we have imagination, fuel for the evolution of man. Knowing how to stay clear or intelligent in a toxic world takes some serious *sight.* This means insight, foresight, hindsight, and recognizing what is on-sight!

As primitive man became more civilized, his desire to stop, *look,* and listen became compromised. The more clever he became with his speech, the more preoccupied he became with seeking the bigger, better deal. This was frequently pursued at the expense of others and served as a breeding ground for ideas identified as "inward," such as anxiety, love, hate, and right or wrong—all of which perpetuated ill intention and the misuse of language. Man's need to heal, sedate, and hide his inner turmoil often produced what we refer to today as "cliques." These communes offered greater sustainability and protection, but members often experienced bestial patterns of thought, a more primitive rendition of man. As man began to push the envelope and think bigger and engage his powers of creativity, a more sophisticated form of fellowship emerged. This was enhanced by language and man's need to find outside solutions to inside problems, where before outside problems took precedence. Primitive man spent little time in his intellect. He was primarily instinctually centered. Today, men have several developed centers, and like primitive man, no two are alike in nature. This aspect of our human nature is more fully discussed in chapter 10.

In an attempt to retrieve the Knowledge of Y.O.U.® (your own understanding) from before the language of man, we must observe language today and how it is used to feed human nature. We as human beings arrive here in our own vehicles, designed to transport our spirits through this lifetime (without an operating manual). The Knowledge of Y.O.U.® helps us retrieve our operating manual. With each generation of human design, new improvements as well as new vulnerabilities are presented. With this advancement in human nature comes the need to communicate more eloquently, fashionably, and intelligently than those that came before us. Unfortunately, man has frequently chosen the more ignorant route in communicating his need to feed upon society. Primitive man did not feed upon the minds and souls of other men, but instead obtained his nourishment from more authentic sources. He did not need to change his story to get what he needed. Today, what may originally have been presented as a simple call to action frequently becomes the latest sensational headline news of disaster. Human beings embroider the truth. We can't help it unless we know how to maintain the integrity of our electromagnetic field, thus allowing our intuition to process information as intelligence. Man has found such great pleasure in embellishing reality that often the original point of concern rarely looks, feels, and operates as originally intended. Consequently, our need to research and mill through various bodies of wisdom seemed the more reasonable method of peeling away the layers to get to the core of truth. This permitted us the opportunity to keep that which could be verified in nature and toss out that which masked the true nature of man. With regard to language, we discovered that much has been unveiled in the unraveling of words and the manner in which they have become twisted, tangled, and spun with self-serving realities and misconstrued truths. Oh, what a tangled web we have woven!

After years of striving to unearth the seed that birthed the first owner's manual of man, a simple, clear language of love—untouched by man-made beliefs, opinions, and societal impositions—has emerged. It is pure, honest, and in alignment with every law of nature, both physical and metaphysical, and easily offers anyone in a relationship of any kind the opportunity to allow it to travel over calm seas.

With the Knowledge of Y.O.U.®, your life's journey will be guided naturally, relieving you of spending unnecessary energy trying to force your way through life. This results in your offering this life the very gift of *you* by simply understanding yourself. You are the lesson. Get *you* and you get it all. You will not have to give anything up, as those aspects that are fixed in us, "our essence," remain in check. Our essence is where our religious beliefs, the records of where we were born and raised, and who our parents are, all live.

In brief, you gain access to your operating manual. You are one of the few people on Earth who get to fully understand how nature shows up in *you* and what that means when it comes to rising to your full potential. Y.O.U.R. (your own understanding resource) *manual* is not like a manual you get at the DMV, your local synagogue, church, spiritual center, temple, or mosque, that provides direction, rules of the road, instruction, and stories of inspiration to guide you on your path through life. Y.O.U.R. manual is something that Mother Nature provides, like the one you find in your automobile's glove compartment. It is specific to *you* and only you. Simply put, the wisdom inherent in the Knowledge of Y.O.U. is derived from the laws of nature and objective understanding. It allows you to truly see that which stands before you in its natural state—in the obvious. In this application of natural understanding, you become in touch with your authentic self.

You are best revealed when described using three physical laws of nature and a very strong metaphysical law of nature. *Meta* simply means *more or beyond*. Once upon a time, people were likely aware of many more laws than we are today, perhaps they even had access to laws that permitted man to easily levitate or walk on water, often thought to be a skill or intelligent understanding of how to regulate the hydrogen of one's physicality. Ancient reports in religion and legend likewise reveal discussions addressing levitation, walking on water, moving mountains, and mind over matter. Perhaps these reports are true and the participants used various lawful applications to achieve these outcomes. Unfortunately, not a lot of tangible evidence is available today. However, we do have tangible examples of fire walks, steel-bending feats, and people who heal themselves with methods that typically defy medical prognosis. Outside of religious doctrine and the manipulated (not-so-obvious) magic acts of David Blaine, Chris Angel, David Copperfield, and others, we find ourselves grasping at man's new and improved reasoning as it applies to managing our energy and our life, and obtaining health, wealth, love, and perfect self-expression. We are constantly searching for the truth about everything, especially the truth of our self. With self-understanding, we gain an understanding of those around us. As long as we continue to sign up for what works for others, we are likely to fall short of meeting our self and honoring our own potential. Everyone is unique. No two of us are alike ... at least not yet.

Your sole responsibility is to come to know *what you are* and *how to operate your self.* Once you get Y.O.U., self-understanding becomes a thing of the past and you can proceed naturally on the road of life, sharing your gifts and talents with the world. These gifts express themselves in two ways. One is a natural talent, a God-given gift not requiring any prerequisite in education. The second is a learned behavior, a talent that reveals itself through repetitive training and perhaps even overriding innate attributes. Understanding what natural and learned behaviors *look* like presents an opportunity to begin *seeing* yourself. Natural talent subscribes to natural or physical law, and the integrity of its outward presentation is contingent on one's ability to maintain its awareness of that which serves as its source.

Natural (visible, physical, and verifiable with the naked eye) laws and supernatural (invisible, metaphysical, and time) laws were both available to that same primitive man standing at the water's edge before language arrived. In fact, our psycho-babble and uninformed methods of feeding ourselves have really messed things up. So much so, that to begin listing and illustrating the course of events in a state of rewind would take decades. It's more important to know that *now* we have some serious untangling to do, and this all must begin with mastering the simplest form of understanding ever known to man. We must enlist the talents of our naked eye. In many ways, where once we could see, we now are blind. It's definitely time to regain our sight, our insight, and our access to intelligence.

With sight, there are no secrets. Secrets are born of ignorance, and ignorance is born of manipulated truth. If something is declared a secret, man has likely touched it with his own issues of lack and fear. Before man could create a secret or covet a secret, others had to value that which he was keeping secret. This display of thought was then leveraged in a manner that afforded him an easier, less natural way of feeding himself. Welcome to the birth of self-servitude and the manifestation of ignorance. Now some may ask, "Didn't primitive man hide things from others, like food, for example?" The answer to this is yes, but his food was acquired intelligently to be used for his own physical survival. The need to seek food and guard it from predatory behaviors was no mystery to men. Intelligence urges man to seek food, share it when possible, and not use it for harmful or manipulative purposes in an attempt to mislead others. This outward demonstration of territorialism and deception is a natural expression of ignorance. Prior to language, there were no secrets as we know them today. We have white lies, speculative theories, conspiracies, rumors, and truths that may not be true. These are frequently used for purposes of mind control and thought reform. If we know who we are and what we are, we have the choice to remain in control and to make conscious (versus unconscious) choices. However, like anything of value, nothing is exempt from being disproved, questioned, or misconstrued. It was not until the birth of words that we began to see the power of keeping others in a state of ignorance. It's at this point in man's development that we began to catch a glimpse of the decline of reason, response, and an interrupted access to intelligence. Later, with the beginning of clearly spoken language—stimulated by pictures that synthesized meaning and thought into one dimension—came the almost complete demise of intelligence in its natural state of purity and intention. Where once man had a clear conscience and connection with intelligence, he now possessed alternatives, choices, and options for a growing dysfunctional appetite. Originally, his intelligence was so strong that it flew by intuition at one hundred and twenty miles per hour like a BMW 740il on the German Autobahn. Intuition is actually a filtering mechanism, allowing intelligence to present itself purely. Now, with all the chatter, opinions, and man-made theories about life, it's a wonder we can hear ourselves at all. Taking in all of this noise is similar to accumulating particles in any filter. Remaining clean and clear is part of this life's challenge. In fact, millions of dollars are being spent on trying to remember how to regain clear access to our own intelligence. Somewhere in the hallowed halls of our own library of ancestry, we can recall a more reasonable time. It's not unusual to hear comments about how fast the world is going by today in spite of all our modern conveniences to better manage it. The desire to have more time to become better acquainted with our self and our family is still a familiar cry. How well do you really know you? Ask yourself this same question of the loved ones in your life. The truth is, life is about relationships and then you die. It doesn't matter if it's a relationship with many, God, or just yourself. At the very minimum, one would think getting to know *you* would be the first order of business. If you can't do it for you, do it for your God and those around you. Just start somewhere. Reading this book is a very good place to begin getting to know *you.*

Chapter Two

Understanding your DOS

Our Divine Operating System's checklist.
How to maintain the integrity of who you are in spite of living in a toxic world.

*I*n today's world, we are faced with having to interpret and understand many languages in order to relate to those around us. Metaphors, similes, and analogies are plentiful in trying to create a practical image for applying natural law to our lives. These applications can be very beneficial from an educational perspective. Conversely, the fact that they even exist for the taking reveals that they hold a great deal of significance when it comes to the matrix of our existence. In trying to identify the layers of our human behavioral character and that which is responsible for its outward demonstration, we must choose an application that best mirrors our performance and its influences. In expressing the components of natural law and the manner in which they present themselves in the human being, one would think selecting something that is living would be most appropriate, but in this case, the most applicable reflection of human nature comes from a manufactured replica of man multiplied by infinity. This would best be described as a computer. In an attempt to educate, plants, animals, cars, and computers serve as relative applications of understanding.

Since most people own a computer or at least understand some of the dialogue relating to computers, the first example will parallel this technology.

Computers are fairly complex, like people, and the possibility of seeing a new and improved edition is inevitable. People, like computers, are evolving as a species. We look or behave nothing like we did 650,000 years ago. Our ability to process, reason, create, and perceive has grown exponentially. The evolution of our species parallels and influences all that exists on the planet today. Additionally, everything is influenced by two laws: the Law of Three and the Law of Seven. The Law of Three is a visible law. It can be seen with the naked eye. The notion that you can't judge a book by its cover is simply not true. God, an infinite intelligence, a universal power, or an unknown source to some, labored over the natural mathematical physical creation of each and every one of us. It is a formula that propagates and becomes enhanced with each unique encounter that serves to unite and in return procreate once again. This process is organically riddled with its own html format. Within us is a source code that allows us to show up on our desktop—best described as our hair color, our skin tone, our musculature, the twinkle in our eye, and all that can be seen as physically obvious. Some of us are heavy in terms of weight. The gravity of our physicality holds meaning. Unfortunately, we as a species cannot see the reality or nature of what it is to be large in size and heavy in nature. Conversely, some of us are light as a feather, and this simple observation means a great deal to those that know what the significance of being lightweight means. Being heavy does not necessarily mean that we are lazy and have little regard for our health. More often than not, we are truthfully looking at an individual who is passive and positive in nature and significantly can hold more wisdom than other individuals smaller in size. Their ability and potential to retain information is greater and frequently more weight shows up as being in direct proportion to volume or rather volumes of information inherent within. The cliché "elephants never forget" is a flippant but honest clue identifying the animal's true nature. Likewise, larger individuals mimic libraries, always absorbing and never forgetting, having access to volumes of recorded history. They are "the wise ones" capable of storing more information and retrieving it effortlessly for future use. Typically, they process information at a slow, thorough, and steady pace. On the contrary, a mouse is quite different. It's curious how Disney's version of Dumbo and his comrade "the mouse" became best buddies. In understanding natural law, we would call them a maximum attraction. Each brought to the table the missing piece of the other. By combining their natural talents of positive and negative electromagnetic perceptivity, we can embrace perfection as it exists in its natural state. Understanding what shows up physically can aid us a great deal in terms of manifesting harmonious relationships in all aspects of life.

Our physical representation, when observed in parts, can best be described as the icons on our desktop. If one were to imagine man as a rather primitive computer, our icons would be descriptors, that which is obvious to the naked eye. Our hair color, eye color, height, weight, skin tone, musculature, and other various characteristics are a reflection of a source code that represents a connection between the two laws. Without the Law of Seven, the Law of Three cannot show up. Without an outside unseen source, we cannot show up. The Law of Seven, unlike the Law of Three, is not as easily seen, and oftentimes it's simply invisible. The seven days of the week are a good example. We know they exist, yet we cannot see Monday or describe what it looks like. This law, as it relates to human performance, is similar to the digital source code of a computer, in that it too cannot be seen, yet it governs performance from behind the scene. However, it is largely responsible for the way in which we show up on our desktop. Without the DOS (disk operating system) of a computer, or the DOS (divine operating system) of our human existence, there would be nothing showing up on our computer's desktop. Identifying the significance of the icons of your own personal existence and mastering the programming of each leads to self-mastery. We all want to show up in a state of perfection. This is what was intended, and yet the strong and weak nuclear forces of this lifetime continue to influence our own personal performance. A lack of clarity or strength compromises our ability to relate and understand ourselves and others. We become imbalanced, and the ability to *show up* and *participate* with integrity *consistently* becomes a fantasy. Eventually, performing in an unhealthy, unnatural way begins to rob us of physical energy. A continued duplication of this distorted reality will generate disease, and when disease sets in, our icons begin to suffer. We simply stop being our "self." We look different, feel affected, and respond unfavorably to all that we encounter. It's as if our DOS encountered a virus, or in some cases, many viruses. Viruses are a by-product of a toxic world.

In the beginning, waters ran clear and the skies offered an invigorating and life-sustaining means of revitalizing man with each and every breath he took. Words did not exist to infiltrate the cells of his body, and in many ways man was not clever. Instead, he was intelligent. He had direct access to the source of his existence, and given that he was able to relate more clearly to nature itself, without the distractions of our lifetime, there was little room for him to experience the level of pollution that we expose our bodies, minds, and spirits to today. Managing the toxicity of this lifetime is as time-consuming as pursuing one's dream. And to convolute the whole matter, the dream is at the direct effect of the toxicity present in a person's life. Consequently, many dreams are not coming true, people are getting sick and tired of life, and the will to thrive is diminishing. Decisions are lacking integrity and reek of self-absorption. This is happening every day to everyone. The irony in all of this is that if we learn how to maintain our DOS, it can be averted and we can come to enjoy a new state of natural health and being. This maintenance process requires that we sign up for checking in with our self three times a day, seven days a week. It was this innate understanding that birthed praying over each meal in expressing gratitude for the meal served morning, noon, and night. Religion was quick to capitalize on this ritual, making it more worthy of attention than perhaps originally intended. In fact, the way in which we maintain the integrity of our DOS is by checking in with the same seven laws that are found in every religion on the face of this planet. When we fail to incorporate these principles of common sense into our daily lives, our electromagnetic field grows weak and we fall prey to toxicity. Simply put, we must make sure that we:

1. Hold a vision of goodness for ourselves and others.

2. Treat others as you would like to be treated.

3. Speak kindly always.

4. Flow in the face of adversity.

5. Forgive everything.

6. Forget all that is forgiven.

7. Love without expecting anything in return.

It's in trying to master these simple truths that we encounter the need for religion and fellowship. Self-mastery comes in understanding why we must meet the demands of the magnificent seven. For without self-mastery, we will continue to blindly experience a life rich in spectacle, literally missing the show.

In sharing what toxicity looks like, I have included some client-advisement scenarios. Many are from my own experience with clients as well as other certified practitioner stories. YCG's Dr. Beth Wade volunteered to transcribe and breathe life into these circumstances so that others may benefit. Each serves to demonstrate the significance The Ultimate Life Tool® technology has to offer when used with clients. Names, dates, places, and intimate details have been changed to maintain confidentiality. It is our hope that those who read this book seeking answers for themselves may come to realize that everyone has a similar story, and moving beyond it with eyes wide open guided by a certified Y.O.U. professional can lead to a life of amazing health, wealth, love, and perfect self-expression, thus granting you the freedom to be *you*.

Derrick, age 20: *Breaking Old Habits*

I was introduced to Derrick, age twenty, at the request of his mother. He seemed to be lost and making poor decisions. He had started and quit two schools. He didn't have a job and wasn't motivated to get one. He preferred to live at home, afraid to assume the new responsibilities of life. He smoked pot daily and claimed he was free to do so, as he was of age. His parents were extremely frustrated, yet they did not feel comfortable kicking him out, as he was ill-prepared to survive and thrive on his own.

As our children reach age eighteen, graduate from high school, and head off on their various adventures, we breathe a collective sigh of relief. We feel as though our job is just about done as they prepare to assume the adult responsibilities of life and self-sufficiency. Although we truly wish this was the case, one of the most critical times of life lies between the ages of seventeen and twenty-five. This seems to be particularly true for young men.

Society deems one an "adult" at age twenty-one. Yet the youth of today, in the perfection of full bloom, are just driving off the showroom floor with very little practical experience in life. This time of independence and inexperience leaves one heading down the road of life without a map. Our youth succumb to poor decisions, peer pressure, over-indulgent music videos, self-mutilation, drugs, sex, alcohol, and fast cars. They demand independence from their parents, yet many live at home. They appear to have a false sense of entitlement and do not assume adult responsibilities. As much as they demand independence, they often continue to cling to parents for assistance in all aspects of life, seemingly unable to navigate the gauntlet before them. They are frozen by fear, yet boast of boldness. They complain about lack of employment, yet sit on the couch getting stoned and playing video games. They bounce from school to school in an attempt to find the right fit. They engage in reckless behavior, disrespect property, and show little regard for their own health or safety. Ahhh, to be young and immortal!

The beauty of The Ultimate Life Tool® for this age range is that it makes our youth aware of their natural gifts. Their personal operating manual is reviewed in detail in a positive, respectful manner, creating a love for self and the ability to make decisions in alignment with their unique talents.

Derrick is clearly not happy about being in my office, but he knows he will not have a place to live if he is not present. I review his assessment results, referring to it as his operating manual, employing the metaphor of a car to help him understand his unique being. Using automobiles to describe personal performance works very well with young men, as it relates to their attraction to fast cars. I explain that his body is the vehicle that transports him through this life. The proper care and maintenance of his vehicle ensures that he will arrive at his destination (goals) intact and in good running order. I query, "Are you a Porsche or a Jeep? Do you require premium or unleaded fuel? Are your tires properly balanced? Who is the driver and co-pilot of your vehicle? Does your vehicle elicit a positive or negative response from others? Do you drive aggressively or are you relaxed and more passive?" Yes, each of these questions pertains to an aspect of this multi-dimensional human assessment tool and the young man who sits before me. And yes, I have his attention.

In sharing his online assessment results, I express, "You have a serene and benevolent presence that naturally becomes you. Others see you as a necessary decision-maker when reaching a consensus. You are able to see the big picture in most circumstances and are able to fashion a solution for the benefit of all concerned. People listen to you. You naturally take on responsibility and are extremely reliable." Derrick sits a bit taller in his chair.

I continue, "You are on a mission, looking for the quickest and most efficient way to get things done. Your goal is to get the job done without interruption. This aspect of you is also quite honorable, with high standards, and will push for those standards if the need arises. You are like a knight needing a crusade. When you are happy, this naturally creates confidence in others through your exuberant and cheerful disposition. You are drawn to experiences and you are somewhat of a walking encyclopedia when it comes to anything of interest. You love to accomplish things, yet fear or apathy is preventing you from exhibiting your greatness to the world. You are compassionate, which means you feel what others around you are feeling."

Derrick interrupts me. "You can see this in me?"

I reply, "I can, and much more!"

He is now sitting bright-eyed, chest out, and he is listening intently. We continue to review his results. As I share the many aspects of his wonderful vehicle, a tear rolls down his cheek. He is filled with joy and a bit overwhelmed that a stranger sitting across from him can "see" him. For the first time, he gets a glimpse of the perfection of his own unique design!

Now we are able to discuss the things in life that excite him. We can match a variety of career choices with his natural capabilities. I was able to share that life happens in steps and both his parents and I are here to support him each step of the way. We talked about finding an educational experience that can blend his need to accomplish things in a timely manner with his natural ability to connect with those around him, perhaps a certificate program in the healthcare industry. Derrick needs to feel the joy of accomplishment in real time. Once on his way, he may choose further education or a work experience.

The Derrick who walked into my office was *not* the Derrick who walked out of my office. He was proud of himself. He was seen and could honor the wonderful aspects of his unique vehicle. He left with a plan that could be accomplished in a timely manner, and he felt good about his future. He was motivated!

Now imagine what a wonderful gift it would be to provide your young adult with their Personal Operating Manual. Your twenties are about experimenting, but the beauty of this technology is that you are given a navigation system to help you move on down the road with energy-efficient ease. Experimenting now becomes about making choices that are in alignment with your perfect self. The alternative is continually having to get your vehicle repaired, because without navigation, you are more likely to crash.

Kim and the Toxic Boss

People come to see me to get over hurdles, both small and large. I am very grateful to be able to utilize The Ultimate Life Tool® technology in bringing clarity to my clients. They are then able to make informed decisions and move forward with their lives.

Kim came to me because she was in conflict with her boss. It hadn't always been that way. Initially, Kim was thrilled to be working for this high-powered, highly visible woman who was involved with the entertainment industry. As her personal assistant, it was Kim's desire to anticipate and meet this woman's needs in business and in juggling her personal affairs. It had been a mutually agreeable situation until her boss began a love affair with another agent. They would attend lavish parties, where they would consume large quantities of drugs and alcohol. Her boss began to come to work extremely tired, forgetful, and in a constant state of despair regarding her new lover's promiscuity with other women. She was unwilling to leave him, because she enjoyed the visibility his connections afforded her. As a result, Kim became her whipping post. Kim would make travel arrangements to meet her exact specification, only to be verbally slain the next day for not doing it correctly. Her boss would walk in, stand over her, and tap her lips with her index finger, saying, "Read my lips! This is *not* what I wanted! What is wrong with you? You've become an idiot!" This was quickly followed by her storming out of the room. On another occasion, Kim's presence was required in a meeting. When she arrived with the requested material and stood quietly, waiting to be recognized, she was belittled in front of the entire meeting. "Excuse me! Why are you here?" the boss asked in a condescending manner. "Put that on the table and leave!" It was all Kim could do to hold her tongue while holding back the tears. She was looking for a new job but was very aware of her employer's power and authority in the industry and wanted to be able to leave with a clean slate. As each day passed, Kim became meeker and more defensive, which only seemed to make matters worse.

When Kim took The Ultimate Life Tool® assessment, it confirmed that she was losing energy. The assessment also indicated that she was engaging in behavior that was inauthentic to her, in order to survive this ugly scenario. Kim's natural ability was to create order, take initiative, and produce a well-thought-out, aesthetically beautiful product. All she wanted was her employer's approval and recognition for a job well done. When their communication began to break down, Kim stubbornly persevered, knowing she was right yet unable to voice her opinion. She was withholding her frustration and desire to physically hurt this woman for her demeaning and embarrassing outbursts. This caused Kim to lose sleep and forfeit her sense of self-worth, which ultimately resulted in dejection and anger. Her physical well-being was at risk, and she had already begun to show early signs of physical disease in trying to overcome the wrath migraine headaches. The madness had to stop!

When clients come to see me, they are aware of their state of compromise. They often come in exhausted, angry, confused, fed up, betrayed, abandoned, or a combination thereof. They usually know the solution to their challenge yet need guidance from an objective party. They seek validation and permission to take the next step to achieve balance and a peaceful state of mind. Utilizing The Ultimate Life Tool® makes them visible to themselves. There it is in black and white. They answered the questions in the assessment, and the results really do paint a very accurate picture of that person's state of strength or weakness.

Everyone, on some level, knows that health is your greatest wealth. It is always in your best interest to surround yourself with a positive environment, especially if you are spending eight hours a day with someone. Kim and I discussed a number of options. She could continue to work with her boss, with the understanding that her boss was very toxic and that her responses would most likely continue to be caustic in nature. Kim could make an appointment to speak with her boss when they were both calm, and express how her behavior was affecting Kim's mental and physical well-being. Kim hoped that if they were unable to come to a meeting of the minds, her boss would give her a good recommendation as Kim sought employment elsewhere. Kim could feed her employer's need for recognition and attention while setting healthy boundaries of mutually respectful behavior. Kim needed to understand this last option had the potential to continue to drain her energy as she made an attempt to fuel her boss's empty energy pool while Kim's own fuel tank was dangerously low. Or Kim could find employment elsewhere and simply resign.

When Kim arrived at work the next morning, she was rested and calm, knowing she had a number of possible solutions in her hip pocket. Her boss came in late, as she was up into the wee hours of the morning after a film debut. She stood over

Kim, and the toxic behavior instantly began. Kim no longer shrank back from the verbal abuse. She knew it had nothing to do with her. She stood up and looked squarely into her boss's bloodshot eyes. Kim calmly stated that she could no longer tolerate her inappropriate and disrespectful behavior. She gave two weeks' notice, asked to be paid for that time, and left.

Kim was overjoyed. She was free from the weight of misery. Her migraine headaches subsided and she was filled with renewed energy. She couldn't believe she had let this go on for so long! She realized her natural gifts and sought employment with someone who also saw and respected her skill set.

Thank goodness The Ultimate Life Tool® can be used to bring clarity and self-respect to so many.

Chapter Three

Knowing What Is on Your Desktop

How you show up naturally
The Mathematics of Nature and how it influences your physical presentation.

*I*n identifying one's authenticity, or rather what is natural, we must first look to nature. This means spending time observing that which is outside of our self. Currently, and prior to this new era of integrated technology, a great deal of time was devoted to looking within, resurrecting the inner child, and revisiting the past.

With the coming of computer technology arrived a new perspective on health management, a new respect for survival and longevity. This infiltrated all aspects of human maintenance, as well as the health and welfare of the planet. As a result, the "Green Movement" re-emerged full force and began to thoroughly investigate the decline of the human species and the causes that contribute to the ensuing state of demise rapidly encroaching upon our innate human potential. Something deep inside every human being began to surface. Even the most irreverent and wasteful personalities have become haunted by a truth that can no longer be dismissed and overlooked as if it were a loud sneeze, potentially hazardous but easily forgotten.

Fortunately, a great deal of attention has been placed on raising the consciousness of this planet. This responsibility is no longer handed off to the spiritually inclined and those who prefer to help through prayer and other passive means of resolution. For the first time in centuries, large numbers of people throughout the world are taking physical action, and it's working! Why is it working? What is it about physicality that makes people, places, and things operate more intelligently? How does physicality differ from meta-physicality? What is physicality?

To answer these very common questions, I would first like to set a precedent. Given that we live on a planet that is three-dimensional in nature and rotates quite effortlessly without any direction from us in the third dimension, would it not make sense that physicality (that which subscribes to the Law of Three) likely governs all that exists physically? Furthermore, recognizing that nothing on the planet is new but simply an improved rendition of an older version, would it not stand to reason that human beings evolve in much the same manner as anything else physical in nature? If we look at anthropological studies identifying the nature of evolution, we will discover subtleties and often dramatic differences in the natural development of plants, trees, animals, humans, terrain, architecture, cars, etc. With the passing of several eras and generations, changes in human potential naturally occur. Individuals wired slightly differently and advanced beyond their years often show up and contribute new discoveries or fall prey to rejection and fail to leave their gift behind once they pass, and if they do not procreate, a delay in evolution occurs. Being able to identify new versions of our self is vital to initiating intelligence on a global scale, and knowing the difference between intelligence and ignorance requires more information before we can ever regain our sight of self. In fact, we are a species that can no longer see itself. We have become blind. I am sure this saddens our Creator to some extent.

Being able to see first begins with the Law of Three, the first concept in understanding the Natural Mathematics of Man®. When we look at one another, we have no clue as to what the color of our eyes or skin tone reveals in terms of our disposition, electromagnetic potential, and purpose. If we dismiss or overlook the stripes on a female tiger, one might mistake her for a lioness, yet the tiger possesses more aggressive territorial behaviors, perceptivity, and physical strength than the lioness. This is revealed by knowing how to see. The stripes on a tiger were not designed for the fun of it, but rather as a symbol of electromagnetic potential. They reveal an eagle eye as far as perceptivity is concerned and an active and stealth-like quickness when it comes to the execution of movement or responding at lightning speed to a threat. The tiger swipes faster and identifies threats quicker. The lioness is not as quick, but being bigger, she can get a lucky punch in and do some serious damage, as she is more heavy-handed, rather than quick. All of this deducing comes from being able to see the stripes on the tiger and knowing what they mean. In evaluating the two mathematically from a natural perspective, the tiger would win. Everything shows up for a reason. We must pay attention to the natural aspects of all that we see, especially in our self and in others. Unfortunately, today, when we participate in an assessment, no one asks us if we have dark hair, blue eyes, or stripes. They prefer guessing at why we behave the way we do and generating baselines that have no basis other than the fact that we are either male or female, or some nationality under the influence of our culture, religion, and upbringing. All of these factors obviously play a role in our behavior, but the question is, "Is our behavior authentic to our *self?*" This can't be answered without understanding the Law of Three.

To best understand the Law of Three, one must know that it is a physical law, not a metaphysical law. It is not "Woo Woo." It is factual, has face value, is visible, and can be verified by actually physically seeing the law in action. This method of reasoning is often referred to as scientific; meaning, it can be verified and validated. All that is scientific embraces the three physical elements of this law. To reiterate, the laws exemplifying the science behind the Law of Three are gravity, electromagnetism, and nuclear force. Three simple laws, when assembled in perfect natural order, create a physical, tangible entity, be it a table or a human being. Once we debut outside of the mother's womb, our physicality is the first to speak to those eyes that lay upon our presentation. Everything physically obvious about us clues them in to our needs of the moment. This same simple acknowledgement of our infantile humanness needs to prevail throughout our lifetime. Unfortunately, words get in the way and often detour the real needs of our existence. Knowing how to see the true nature of someone is the first step in meeting their needs. Once we can meet the needs of others, reciprocity takes place, and we naturally take care of our self and each other. This marks the beginning of intelligence manifest. In fact, the three-dimensional world in which we live thrives on the Law of Three. All that operates intelligently enlists this law. Additional examples of the governing Law of Three include morning, noon, and night; red light, yellow light, green light; three strikes you're out; third time's a charm; and three warnings you are fired. These are just a few, as anything that is of value to this physical dimension must subscribe to this law. It takes three trimesters to bring a healthy human into the world. When we fall short of this, we must create a mock womb environment in which the premature little one can succeed in becoming a healthy reality. Understanding this law in depth can change the way we conduct business in love and life. It can be the determining factor in achieving success. There is nothing worse that getting stuck in the Law of Two—the "pipe dream." It is in mastering the Law of Three that we can begin to *see*.

Seeing each other begins with the obvious. Ask yourself, "If I were a computer, what is on my desktop?" Let's see ... You may have big blue sparkly eyes, blonde hair, freckles, fair skin, long fingers, long legs, and a round button nose; or perhaps you have lots of wavy black hair, darker skin, small penetrating brown eyes, and a thick waist. These qualities that identify your physical presence did not show up by mistake. *They mean something!* Everything that shows up and is available to the naked eye means something. Every color, whether it's displayed on a pantone color chart or on the face of a landscaped countryside, has its purpose in revealing the true nature of a person, place, or thing. The same is true when observing a person's size. Some of us are slight and frail, while others are excessively large and sturdy. This identifies our gravitational significance, and with it comes a disposition, meaning we may be more or less predisposed to passive or aggressive behavior. The intricacies of understanding the mathematics of man are vast and cannot be condensed, dumbed down, or homogenized to deliver an instantly gratifying quick fix in determining what we are looking at. It takes time to learn about the programs that sit upon your desktop, and no two desktops are completely alike. They are all custom-made. Sometimes the slightly cooler color of blue in the eyes is all it takes to move someone from being *seen* as an active negative disposition to a positive passive modus operandi. We are all unique! This means no two of us are alike. We have no business telling someone to try what worked for us with the same level of confidence that it will work for another. All too often, we fail in prescribing solutions simply because we are blind to *what* stands before us. It is very similar to being an auto mechanic and having someone drive their vehicle in for maintenance or repair. As mind, body, and spiritual mechanics, we open up our tool kit and begin using tools that may or may not be appropriate for the type of vehicle we are working on; much like putting Cadillac Escalade auto parts on a Mercedes 550SL. This being said, it is vital that we as human beings raising other human beings, specifically our own children, assume responsibility in knowing what we are looking at and what is naturally best for them. Typically, we like to prospect strategic truths and solutions that worked for us as children, only to find that often the child rebels in response to feeling unseen, misunderstood, or disrespected. For some people, respect is a prerequisite, equal to or greater than love. However, this is not the case for everyone. We must ask ourselves, how can we be sure to properly acknowledge, respectfully address, and love unconditionally that which we cannot fully identify?

Just for a minute, imagine that all animals can talk. Let us say that Mr. Lion, king of the forest, has decided to take the health and welfare of all the animals in the forest under his control. Wanting to do right by all of them, he chooses to seek a career in counseling so that he may assist them in rising to their full potential. Additionally, he decides to create a more species-appropriate assessment instrument in delivering his counseling services. Assuming he has the same insightful skills as humans today, he realizes that he must rely on answers and actions, rather than knowing what his clients are, as seen through the eyes of Mother Nature. He, like most people today, has bought into the fallacies, "you can't judge a book by its cover" and "appearances can be deceiving," both of which can be substantiated through blind examples riddled with missing information. Now, being a lion, raised by wonderful lion parents with loving lion values, he begins to formulate his questions. The first very important question is, "Do you roar?" followed by question number two, "Do you eat meat?" Subscribing to a binary coding system, he feels strongly that a yes answer will very accurately identify a healthy disposition and a healthy physical state, both of which, he feels, should result in a robust and aggressive behavior, destined for success. Upon completion of his instrument, he hangs his shingle out for business. In walks, or rather hops, his first client, Mr. Bunny.

Mr. Bunny is asked to first take the assessment. He is then seated in Dr. Lion's office (he decided to get his PhD), where his results will be discussed one on one. Upon reviewing Mr. Bunny's results and identifying that he has clearly lost his voice and is suffering from low self-esteem and likely anemia, compounded by physical fatigue due to a lack of red meat, Dr. Lion advises that he purchase a block of sessions totaling four thousand bushels of carrots. Dr. Lion further reassures Mr.

Bunny that he will have him running football fields at lightning speed and screaming from the mountaintops in no time at all. Mr. Bunny, not having any luck with his own strategies (suffering from an identity crisis and depression) figures the kindly doctor surely knows what he is doing. Mr. Bunny proceeds to participate in recommended voice-enhancement practices and switches from carrots to meat. Headline news soon after reported Mr. Bunny was pronounced dead on arrival three weeks later from an intestinal hemorrhage. He tried to yell for help, but he had acquired a severe case of laryngitis. Consequently, help did not arrive in time. Clearly, this could have been avoided. It happened because he was not seen and could not be heard. Dr. Lion did not know what he was looking at. This juvenile story is not that far-fetched when compared to the grown-up stories we hear today, addressing people seeking answers for self-preservation and fulfillment. Until we regain our ability to authentically recognize each other, we will continue to misunderstand and poorly advise one another as friends, family, experts, and colleagues. It's a bit of a crap shoot. Sometimes we will be right and sometimes we will be wrong. Unfortunately, we often make the "what worked" scenario a norm for everyone. Just because watering an oak tree produces a healthy response does not necessarily mean that equally watering a paloverde tree or a saguaro cactus will result in the same outcome. Again, we need to know what we are looking at.

It is in the needing to know that we, as a species, have acquired more than three thousand psychometric tools. These instruments assess that which lies beneath the surface of our physicality and, if taken seriously, can identify behavioral qualities that may or may not be authentic to an individual. Sometimes dusting the toxicity of life off is all that is required to restore a healthy presentation of self. The Ultimate Life Tool® technology offers a place for all of the current psychometric tools to reside, thus adding tremendous value to one's perception of human reality. By knowing *what* is taking the test—as in the case of Mr. Bunny and Dr. Lion—the answers derived from an assessment have greater meaning and oftentimes tell a different story than when looking at a one-dimensional, multi-faceted instrument as the only means of deduction. The Ultimate Life Tool® technology is a multi-dimensional tool that offers a single physical (three-dimensional) image of a human being, revealing *what* the person is and how innate multidimensional qualities interface. It is the interface that distinguishes the significance of our uniqueness, coupled with the gravitational qualities of our style or physical presentation of self. When you know where the answers to current popular assessment instruments live, reality becomes obvious. Whether you choose to enlist the Ultimate Life Tool® as the only means of diagnosing human reality or choose to use it as a foundation from which to glean a more realistic, in-depth perception of yourself or your client, it is imperative that this technology be the first tool of choice. Again, success is likely if you know *first* what you are dealing with, versus just knowing how something or someone is behaving. A kitten that roars and a lion that meows would be perceived accurately as weak behavior if one could *see* what was doing the behaving. As a life advisor, parent, employer, or friend, the technology tells you what will walk in the door and how strong or weak they are, prior to coming in. This provides a head start in addressing needs more accurately, versus wasting valuable time overlooking the obvious, revisiting yesterday, and listening to rhetoric that has little to do with optimizing their natural physical performance.

I'll never forget the first time Dr. Charles Richards came to my home. Having heard about my work, he arrived curious about the technology and its promise for the future. Being quite the expert himself, licensed in psychology and having served as one of CCL's (the Center for Creative Leadership) finest assessment analysts for eleven years, he was elated at the brevity and accuracy of the ULT technology. In fact, he joined our board of directors in supporting the growth and significance of the knowledge. This kind of participation and support arrives daily, and we are always appreciative of the organic enfoldment that has presented itself with little advertising or promotion. Dr. Richards has been noted as saying, "After spending eleven years working with Fortune 500 executives, as a trainer and feedback consultant at the Center for Creative Leadership (CCL), I've found YCG's assessment instrument to be one of the most comprehensive I've used. With one brief questionnaire, its results combine the breadth and depth of eight to ten instruments previously used for personality assessment, team-building, and overall organizational development. I highly recommend it for those seeking a comprehensive, cutting-edge, individual and group assessment tool."

If you are a relationship expert in the business of promoting human mental health, you owe it to your clients to fully understand the nature of what they are.

With this technology, you are given a pair of glasses with which to see them. When I first spoke about the knowledge in the foreword of this book and the scientist, Nanz Zekela, who came up to me in awe at the gift this provides, I felt very much alone. I was the only person who could see using natural law. It was her suggestion to convert the knowledge into a user-friendly technology that permits others to see without having to master a new language. This really excited me, because I knew it would take several years to teach someone to *see* like I do, but with the technology and a small investment of time and money, anyone can see.

The Law of Three is supported by the Law of Seven. Each represents the integral parts of the Natural Mathematics of Man®. In summation, we are looking at a base-ten reality, often called the metric system, the only real universal language on the planet. It is this same mathematical formula that supports science in quantifying all that is reasonable from the quark to the cosmos.

Chapter Four

Mother Nature's Rocks and Water

The True Nature of Men and Women
Revealing your purpose unto one another and beyond.

We, the human race, spend billions of dollars trying to sort through male and female differences in developing methods of understanding and relationship management. The first obvious truth lies in knowing that women represent a physical expression of Mother Nature in the way they are designed to manage the relationships of this lifetime. They are created to expand and move, to give birth, and multitask. Unfortunately, women have become confused over thousands of years, and many have forgotten their role in this lifetime and the significance they play in maintaining the whole. They fear they must give something up or lose themselves to laundry and a life of less. This is not true. However, if women continue to ignore their role in nature, men will become restless, diseased, and deteriorate before our eyes from lack of attention on their part. It is Mother Nature who bathes the sharp, jagged rock in the bottom of the stream until it becomes smooth and rounded. She doesn't pound it, sand it, or rub it till it's raw, while making demands and laying down expectations. Her touch is kind and loving. It is the mother who shares her ocean of serenity so that relationships may travel over a calm sea. In every

43

aspect of our existence, both present and previous, it is the mother who holds the recipe for life and how to sustain it. It is a woman's responsibility to keep the relationship clean and healthy. Even in our world of computer technology, where man has developed an exponential prototype to assist the physical world, we find that it, too, is completely reliant on the health and performance of the "motherboard." There is nothing new on this planet. The laws are *always* the same. They never change, and they apply to everything that exists in this three-dimensional world. Mankind simply fails to follow them.

Mankind's various expressions are no accident, revealing themselves in popular quotations, clichés, and words of wisdom such as "don't bite the hand that feeds you," "third time is a charm," and "don't rock the boat." Natural trends and popular clues emerge every day to remind us of our forgotten nature. We must look for the mother in what is spoken or what stands before us as an opportunity or suggestion. Intelligence always speaks through the mother, meaning it can be verified in nature. It is the mother's love that is most revered in every era of man. It is the innate understanding, the uninterrupted fragment of intelligence that remains intact and ever present in our hearts that permits us to honor that which gives birth. Still, women sign up for all kinds of self-improvement workshops and ideas that take them further from acknowledging their role. This does not mean they must adopt the recommendations of parenting authorities or accept guilt trips from family members. Instead they should enlist the laws of nature to better determine what is best for them and for those who live in and around their environment. Mother Nature knows best, and as we all know as stated by a famous margarine manufacturer, "It's not nice to fool Mother Nature".

Oftentimes, popular icons, gurus, and wannabe authorities find an opportunity and try to fill Mother Nature's shoes, but they only create confusion and separation. Mother Nature left us physical landmarks to guide us. She gave us many obvious impressions of how to recognize what is right and what is inappropriate, reminding us that the laws of nature impose different guidelines and recommendations for each and every living thing that exists on the planet. No two entities require the same kind of care or treatment when it comes to optimizing their performance in this lifetime. It would be like putting diesel fuel in a car that required premium unleaded. In chapter one, we referenced the cactus and the pine tree. Each required a different environment and circumstances in order to thrive. Unfortunately, we suffer from mass homogenization and have come to believe that one treatment is good for all. Quick fixes and abbreviated versions of how and when to embark upon your perfect life journey flood the market. For example, learning a foreign language like Spanish takes time. Survival Spanish will only get you so far, meaning sooner or later you are going to keep coming up short of communicating efficiently. Successful communication will ultimately require that you put in the time, energy, and practice to learn the language in its entirety. Likewise, the bits and pieces we grasp of physical and metaphysical understanding by subscribing to the latest self-help fads simply provide us with enough information to do a whole lot of damage. We sound intelligent, when in fact we are basically dangerous. And worse yet, people will follow the partially informed, while the partially informed often cease to grow, thinking they know it all. This is why it is so important to know *you*. If you only come to understand one thing in this life, let it be you. This is the primary request of every healthy mother, hoping and holding the vision that her child will rise to his or her full potential.

Again, remembering health is our greatest wealth, and knowing this, we need to honor that which sustains us, Mother Earth—that powerful yet feminine presence that can bathe and calm the savage beast. When describing the significance women play in the scheme of things, it is best to reference nature and the math behind the universal principle that defines survival. In brief, women are like water and men are like rocks. YCG has created Rocks and Water Seminars devoted to helping individuals better understand the difference between men and women, as well as their contribution to one another. It's important that we come to understand that Mother Ocean covers 70 percent of this planet, leaving the remaining 30 percent dedicated to land and mountains. When addressing the physicality, the male and female attributes of this planet, it is best said, "It is Mother Earth, Mother Nature, and Mother Ocean. It is Father Time and *king* of the mountain ... not *queen*." If a mountain receives no water or moisture, there is no growth. Trees and flowers do not flourish, and eventually the king begins to crumble, disintegrate, or become petrified. Should a man become petrified from having experienced moisture-deprived relationships, it could result in what appears as "fear of commitment." Many men today are conditioned to believe that there is a greater chance of staying nourished by not committing. We see this as divorce rates climb from not having tools of understanding. Divorce is a by-product of misunderstanding and malnourishment. Always! Oftentimes, women have been taught that they are to be served rather than serve, when in fact a woman's role is to *move,* and the man's is to offer stability and reliance. He grounds the relationship and she keeps it moving forward and clean. Neither role implies that one is required to make more money or neglect their responsibilities. Each must work together, for without assuming these roles, the Earth crumbles into a massive mud puddle. In fact, most relationships are *muddy!* Gaining an understanding of one's personal nature through the Knowledge of Y.O.U.® coupled with The Ultimate Life Tool® technology saves relationships and brings clarity. It's like going through a car wash; all of sudden you can *see* where you are going, and it only took *water.*

In revisiting this feminine significance, the woman holds the key to the family dynamics. She grows things inside, outside, and all around her. When we look at spiritual and religious philosophy, we consistently hear similar scriptural reports that "it is the woman who tears down the walls of the home." This statement is not to make woman out to be the villain, but rather to illustrate her powerful significance in demonstrating the control or lack of control in managing *life.* She sustains life! We see this with the lioness and her cubs. Were she to get upset with her mate and march off, the cubs would suffer and possibly die. With man, widowed males left to raise newborn infants seek feminine assistance and expertise in meeting the baby's needs. They don't call their dads! They regularly seek out their mother, aunt, grandmother, sister, or the neighbor lady for advice.

Women are so powerful that when relationships are falling apart in every facet of life, one can often trace the dysfunction back to a woman. Sometimes it's a refusal to bathe the sharp, pointed rock that sets off a chain reaction that spills over into the office clerk's world, who barks at the grocery store clerk, who takes it out on her kid, who goes to school the next day and gets expelled for having purposely tripped a little girl on the playground. When we go to the very core of corruption, the abuse of power lies with the woman. Crimes and injustices of every kind could have been averted by a loving mother. Men enforce the law. Women, when doing their job, practice *the law.* Specifically, the law of nature authored by … guess who? *Mother Nature.* This law heals, feels, and reveals the *truth* of man. Without water, there is *no* electricity. She is power. Today, our Mother Earth is dying from toxicity, and she is sending out a plea to all women to rise up and acknowledge their significance.

Oftentimes, a situation is easily misunderstood. In the following case studies, one can gain an understanding of how people can improve their relationships by sorting through the minutia of life's challenges.

Ray and Carmen: *Couple in Crisis*

I listened as Carmen sobbed and Ray stared into space. She was filled with hurt, disappointment, and fear. "I feel so betrayed. We have spent the last seven years building a life together and he chooses to throw it all away."

As a trained life advisor, I have been privy to this type of dilemma and similar scenarios as marriages crumble and dreams of life, home, and success fade when one partner is not being fed. It was clear that what they needed in order to stay alive within the marriage was not available. Fortunately, through The Knowledge of Y.O.U.® and the Ultimate Life Tool® technology, I am able to frequently help couples in crisis navigate to calmer waters.

Ray and Carmen were thirty-four and thirty respectively. They had met each other at a party and soon after fell in love and moved in together. Renting a small, inexpensive two-bedroom condo afforded them the opportunity to build their business while saving for a home. They decided to get married when Carmen became pregnant. When their first child arrived, Carmen asked her mother to move in, to help with the baby while she and Ray ran the business. Carmen was great at creating order, and this seemed like a logical solution. She didn't have to be concerned about a daycare provider. This allowed her to work and come home to check on the baby, giving her mother a moment of relief. Her plan seemed to be working, and she and Ray pressed on. Babies two and three soon followed, filling their two-bedroom, one-bath condo with overwhelming activity. Money was tight, so Ray decided to become a bouncer at night to help with the cash flow. He loved Carmen, but with the many stresses of life and a demanding schedule, the two of them found little time to satisfy the natural needs of love and life. It was difficult for them to create alone time. They would work all day, return to a busy home to make dinner, bathe the kids, and put them to bed. Many evenings, Ray would take off to work, leaving these responsibilities to Carmen, who fell into bed exhausted.

Ray naturally required more physical attention and recognition than Carmen. Carmen felt invigorated daily by organizing the demands of work and home. This fed her and kept her going. Ray, on the other hand, needed personal attention in order to thrive. He frequently desired intimacy, but Carmen often refused him, feeling inhibited by having her mother always within earshot. Consequently, Ray's need for attention went unfulfilled more often than not. And to complicate matters, he was juggling two jobs, a busy household, and privacy issues at home. His starved emotional needs were quickly manifesting as seeds of resentment.

Ray's role as a bouncer, supervising the nightclub scene, became a welcome part of his life. He was able to get away from the chaos of home and enter a playground where he received lots of attention. Before long, Ray began to absorb the toxicity of this nightlife. Drugs, alcohol, and beautiful women were plentiful. Gradually, all of his needs were being met, and his family life began to suffer. Carmen sensed his disconnect but continued to manage the growing demands of motherhood and work. Eventually, overwhelming fatigue set in, and her ability to stay revitalized on her own by keeping things organized was not enough. She missed Ray but chose to forge ahead, holding the vision that their diligence would soon pay off. She could see their new life on the horizon. They would live in a larger home, have more room, and she and Ray would have the privacy they required to reconnect.

One evening while Ray was working, Carmen decided to re-organize their closet; inside, she came across a manila envelope stuffed between two sweatshirts. Curious, she opened it to view its contents. She was devastated by the photos inside. Ray was clearly violating the vows of their marriage. Disappointment, insecurity, and humiliation filled the moment. They had so much invested in their business, family, and one another. As hurt and angry as she was, Carmen wasn't sure if she was willing to throw it all away. She called me for help. I suggested that Carmen and Ray take The Ultimate Life Tool® assessment, which helps to identify levels of toxicity and the direction to take for a clearer mindset.

I explained to them that the assessment identifies why we do the things the way we do and what provokes dysfunction. And, furthermore, being that we are all unique requires that we understand one another's differences in meeting the needs of survival. Knowing what moves them forward without draining their batteries would better prepare them to make positive and purposeful decisions in repairing their marriage. More importantly, they would come to realize that the disease of their relationship is not their fault, it's everyone's. With external temptation at an all-time high, it's difficult to stay clear and thwart off ignorance. Each had simply fallen prey to the toxicity of this lifetime.

Clearly, both were frustrated and tired because their needs were not being met. Life was not fun anymore. Aside from the obvious, Carmen was at home in the evening and Ray was gone. The first thing I suggested was that Ray quit his second job as a bouncer. He needed to become a celebrity at home. Both needed to make spending time together a priority. Recognizing that the funds derived from his night job were to be applied toward the purchase of their home seemed unrealistic, given that the marriage was falling apart in pursuit of this goal. Additionally, if Carmen's mother was to remain a part of their household, they needed to move sooner, rather than later, to a larger home with the mother's room at the opposite side of the house. This could require that they rent instead of purchase a home. In the meantime, scheduled date nights were essential. I suggested adding to the evening by occasionally getting a hotel room, a small expense to save a marriage, realizing that a divorce costs considerably more. This would allow Carmen the privacy she needed to fully connect with her husband without inhibition and fulfill their mutual emotional and physical needs.

Fortunately, Carmen and Ray are doing well and their marriage is thriving. Both are grateful for the simple and straightforward advice I was able to share with them. Each now possesses a fundamental understanding of how they operate and what that means in maintaining a healthy marriage.

Prince Not-so Charming

A lovely woman by the name of Jessica came to my office complaining of depression and lack of energy. She felt a bit conflicted by these feelings, as she was a newlywed coming up on her first year of marriage. Jessica was twenty-six years old and had previously dated several men but committed to none. She had been waiting for the perfect Prince Charming. Michael met the majority of requirements on her wish list. He was handsome, had a good job, and could support her if she chose not to work. He came from a good family, and they blended well with hers. He demonstrated respect for her and was kind and generous as well. She loved Michael. Shortly after their wedding, they moved to a beautiful new dream home about forty-five minutes away from their old stomping grounds and familiar friendships.

Jessica believed it was her responsibility to honor Michael and submit to his authority. She felt it was important to run most of her decisions past him before acting. All of this fit into her personal philosophy and her religious values. However, she was quickly losing her identity, as Michael monopolized most of her time and exhibited signs of extreme possessiveness. He would check in on Jessica at regular intervals throughout the day, wondering where she was and with whom. She felt as though she was now his property. Even though this behavior was restrictive and irritating to Jessica, his inquiries also made her feel loved and protected. She was aware that within the first year of marriage there can be many adjustments, but she thought she should be feeling happier and more fulfilled now that her dream had come true. After all, she was living with her handsome prince.

When Jessica took the Ultimate Life Tool® assessment, we discovered that she indeed was experiencing an identity crisis. At age twenty-six, she should be fully present and thriving, yet her energy was dangerously low. Instead of thriving in her environment and relationship, she was languishing. In this weakened state, it was difficult for her to think clearly and make positive changes without assistance. It was obviously necessary to help Jessica identify what fueled her and gave her energy.

In seeking a solution for her, I asked Michael to take the assessment as well. The results revealed that Michael and Jessica were quite well suited for one another. He was very capable of offering the physical and emotional support that she needed to thrive. In attempting to explain what was necessary to improve her current state of being, I expressed that Jessica needed more opportunities to move freely about. Serving her community would be one way in which she could experience opportunities to utilize her talents, thus increasing her self-esteem. Self-esteem issues often manifest as an identity crisis. Given that Michael and Jessica were in a new neighborhood, both needed to make new meaningful connections and friendships. Jessica's first step was to find a ladies' gym, where she could exercise and meet people. This would also increase her self-esteem and begin to restore her energy. Michael was asked to practice trusting her love by loosening his hold on her during the day. They agreed to check in with one another midday, recognizing that they would get to see each other when he got home from work.

We looked at her personal belief system of submitting to her husband. In its truest form, it was all about loving and respecting your partner. Jessica had taken this to an extreme. As a result, she had lost herself. Her desire to love and support Michael was well intended, yet had not played out in a healthy manner for her. Jessica realized she could honor her husband and he would actually enjoy her more if she had projects and friendships outside of their marriage.

I also suggested that Jessica continue to take responsibility for replenishing her energy. Her first priority was to create a quiet place where she could exercise her gift for listening. In addition, I further recommended listening to music or learning how to play an instrument. My reasoning was revealed in the statistics provided through her assessment results. Jessica becomes vital in a more solitary environment and connects easily with her world through sound. In a weakened state, she becomes starved for attention and begins to neglect herself. The results also identified that both Michael and Jessica shared a motivational characteristic that requires space and the ability to sit quietly and listen. While Jessica frequently focused her energy on Michael's needs, it was important for Michael to take a break from this state of being and actively pay attention to Jessica. This would offer her support and recognition, which in turn would bring new energy to the relationship.

In following up with Jessica and Michael on a monthly basis, we were able to identify group activities that they both enjoyed together. This allowed them to forge new friendships as a by-product of their growing relationship. In brief, using The Ultimate Life Tool® allowed us to identify several ways to better improve the health of this marriage.

Chapter Five

Father Time's Natural Order

The Natural Cycle of Life
Admitting we have a "physical" shelf life and understanding the natural order influencing our own personal physical growth and decline.

What if you knew yesterday what you know today? Would you like to turn back the hands of time? Why is it that man often feels lost in knowing what is right for him? In this chapter, we will explore that which chronicles the nature of man's physical existence, looking at the timely details that continuously influence our decisions and our efficiency in carrying out hopes and dreams. The good news is, we don't have to look far to find answers to why things happen when they do. Everything that exists on this planet is a clue revealing a piece of valuable insight that mirrors our own ability to optimize our performance. If we can see it, we are privy to something of great personal value. The worth is portrayed in the very fact that it has manifested physically, and therefore we can call it verifiable and real, a reality. It has fulfilled its purpose in subscribing to physical law, meaning what we are experiencing is gravity, electromagnetism, and nuclear force firsthand. Being able to identify these aspects of physical law in all things visible brings one closer to better understanding the true nature of man. Unfortunately, we are not taught how to identify the reality or truth revealed by physical law in human beings, but rather the importance it plays in creating technology and managing the astronomical effects of war or peace and our own significance in a solar system. Animals, on the other hand, are privy to the role that physical law plays in managing their reality when it comes to survival. In many ways, they are more intelligent than man, and in many ways are less threatened by ignorance, a by-product of toxicity.

Like animals, plants, cars, cities, empires, and eras, human beings have a physical shelf life. Human nature has its own language in relating this alpha/omega concept and is best described by once again referring to the role that the mother and father play in maintaining the integrity of man's arrival, growth, and death. Think about it—without a mother-father contribution, you wouldn't exist. Knowing the role each plays in the nature of our existence is very important when it comes to human understanding. In chapter four, we addressed details identifying the differences between men and women and their objective role in a physical world, as it is mirrored by all that is exemplified in nature. While Mother Nature serves as a governing authority over our ability to heal, feel, and reveal our self, Father Time ticks away as we wander about in our search for answers. Understanding the human cycle of life as it relates to the natural mathematics of man is just like learning how to tell time. It gives you opportunities to maximize your potential by making conscious choices in a timely manner. These choices are founded in realizing the dynamics of the interval you are in and by acknowledging the interval that lies ahead. Little or no energy should be spent on that which has passed. Focusing on the moment and knowing what lies ahead breeds acceptance and allows one to embrace growing up and growing old, as well as cultivating a new perception of what it is to respect everything that is human. This sense of decency serves as the impetus for wanting to understand how to spend the time in between as it relates to our own uniqueness. Getting to know Y.O.U. is one of the most loving gifts you can give yourself and those around you. Once you know what time it is, you cease to challenge it. Consequently, questions fall away, answers simply appear, and you begin to accomplish more by spending less. Sometimes the answer is to just wait a year or two, and sometimes the answer is to act quickly, so as not to struggle once the next interval commences. Fully understanding the nature of Father Time makes the wait endurable, and in many cases, it offers solace in relieving one of something they have no control over. How many times have you fretted over what may or may not happen tomorrow? We are no different than a seed in nature, recognizing it too has no control over its debut above the ground. Mother Nature and Father Time have taken on this regulatory assignment.

In utilizing the technology that serves to support the Knowledge of Y.O.U.®, trained practitioners look at many things, one of which is where the client or individual is at in The Cycle of Life™. The Cycle of Life™ looks exactly like an alarm clock. This is no surprise, for everything physical that exists on this planet is again a clue reflecting all we need to survive in being healthy, wealthy, and wise. This man-made device is intelligence manifested and is not here to just give us input in influencing our decisions with regards to governing our day but also to remind us that we as physical human beings are held accountable by a similar physical reality that repeatedly reminds us of our shelf life. This, in many ways, is far more important than the watch on our wrist. The Knowledge of Y.O.U.®, in revealing The Cycle of Life™ or rather man's watch, chronicles the distinct hallmarks of growth and the need for physical awareness through our own ability to be *on watch* as we grow. Seeing and acknowledging the obvious changes that take place in a child, teenager, and adult is as telling as observing the nature of a rose as it blooms in time for Sunday's centerpiece.

In describing The Cycle of Life™, it is best to rely on a few different kinds of metaphors and analogies. Whether we are describing a plant emerging from a seed to a bud, a car being assembled from a single bolt to leaving the showroom floor, or a caterpillar emerging as a butterfly, everything in this physical life is telling us something about our own physical evolutionary transitions. In *watch*ing a human's evolution, we will see the role that intelligence plays in maintaining the integrity of each interval and ultimately the mathematical formula that repeats itself throughout all material aspects of this lifetime. Let's face it, not everyone had a great childhood, not everyone has a successful marriage, and not everyone lives beyond fifty. However, everyone comes in with potential for success and failure in all of these situations. Learning how to maximize one's experience in each interval of life can enhance it, extend it, and often allows others a chance to embrace the gifts of purpose to be left behind, once the clock stops ticking. The Cycle of Life™ is but one part of The Knowledge of Y.O.U.® encompassing many aspects of the nature of each physical component as it blooms and wilts, expands and contracts, and ebbs and flows throughout the life of man.

Before we begin to address each interval, it is best to provide the diagram used to train professionals in acquiring a deeper understanding of man's alarming nature. On the following page is an illustration of The Cycle of Life™. Please note the similarity between our everyday alarm clock and the image that depicts our shelf life. Similarly, there are twelve intervals that govern our lifetime. We see this formula repeated in the twelve months defining a year and in our distinctions between the clearly defined two sets of twelve hours that separate the AM and PM of our day. While each of us is unique in our own personal design and natural presentation, the element of time that dictates our tomorrow is the same. Time came before us and will continue after we leave. It is not dependent on us, but our self-mastery of this existence is closely predicated by time as defined by man. Understanding the physics and simple quantum layers that prevail allows us to dismiss all of the subjective reasoning that frequently emerges as a part of man's need to excuse himself in making poor choices. In brief, we are being watched in a sense, and that being said, it is wise that we know *how* to watch as well. In many respects, learning how to "tell time" can set us free from our own self-induced imbalance.

THE CYCLE OF LIFE

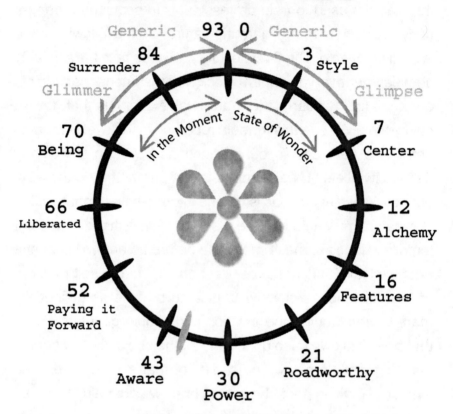

Generic   93 0   Generic
84
Surrender   3 Style
Glimmer   Glimpse

In the Moment   State of Wonder

70   7
Being   Center

66   12
Liberated   Alchemy

16
Features

52
Paying it
Forward

43   21
Aware   30   Roadworthy
Power

Hands of Time

Beginning with age zero and proceeding through each interval until we reach ninety-three, one can see the benchmarks of man's natural evolution. Many will think that they have already experienced an interval prematurely, thus allowing them to skip one later on. But, like everything in the universe, the clock keeps ticking and has yet to jump from 1 PM to 7 PM. This consistency is something we must respect. Fully understanding The Cycle of Life™ as it reveals man's timely nature makes us better human beings.

Age zero to three is commonly referenced as a generic state. This is because there is some question as to just what we are looking at. When observing babies in a nursery, wrapped tightly in flannel receiving blankets so as to feel safe in a big, new world, we often mistake the boys for the girls and vice versa. Unless, of course, they are our own or are lying naked before us. Babies from a physical glance cannot be seen as much more than a sprout above the ground. They only possess two of four energy centers that can connect with the outside world, and seek only being held, fed, and changed.

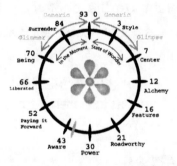

Age three to seven is when we begin to notice *what* we are looking at. If humans were flowers, we would be able to begin to distinguish what family of flowers they belonged to by merely examining the bud that has just begun to show up. Perhaps it is a rose or a ranunculus? Both of which are very similar in appearance.

As the child approaches age seven, we begin to identify more blooming physical traits, all of which point to distinct characteristics of electromagnetism, potential nuclear strengths, and gravitational dispositions. We are not looking for cultural or racial traits, but instead we are looking for more objective clues. Height, skin tone, hair volume, and eye color are just a few physical characteristics that tell us something about their behavior and their potential. When we look at an eagle versus a hummingbird, we know what to expect, and with this knowledge, we know even more about how they think and what motivates them. In the photos on the following page, trained Y.O.U. professionals can easily see this child of three is a passive, positively charged individual with a propensity to be extremely sympathetic in her approach to life. Knowing your child like this can free you to parent him or her effectively until age twenty-one.

She is the type of human that requires a nap midday, regardless of whether she is three or twenty-one. This is not the case for every child or adult.

Children in the three to seven interval are best educated through social means and should not be expected to entertain academic concepts or read unless it is part of a social experience. In today's world, there is an urgency to educate our children academically prematurely. This is done in hopes to set them up for greater success in the years to follow. Often, this need is exacerbated by social pressures placed upon the parents, each needing to be perceived as informed and qualified by others outside of their own nuclear family. Unfortunately, today we have many sixteen-year-olds with no social skills, and one cannot repeat the dynamics of a previous interval once it has passed. As in all things relying on nature, there is a natural order of organic enfoldment that must take place in which the thing receives the gift of growth. For example, if a child at age four spends her time learning a foreign language, mathematical concepts, and fundamentals of reading in an intellectual classroom setting, rather than learning them circuitously through play and socialization, her intellectual center will become over-inflated, and her chance to develop social skills will become permanently impaired. Should she enter a charm school later on, the subject matter will feel foreign and uncomfortable and rob her of energy. When we have to learn something that is unnatural or out of order, it creates struggle, denies us mastery, and is not energy efficient. Children naturally learn to be kind, share, and become purposeful in this interval. To miss this is to violate the laws of human nature as it clearly produces less desirable outcomes later on down the road.

Age seven to twelve clearly reveals how a child learns and relates to his or her environment. All four centers are ready for reception and transmission by age seven. This is when academia can be officially introduced. In addition, more physical traits are revealed and signs of passivity or active tendencies become more pronounced. In providing in-services for education, teachers are embracing this concept, as they now have a tool that allows them to see how a child learns. Even more importantly, they come to realize how their own pronounced energetic delivery impacts children who are wired differently. Eventually, this knowledge will change the face of education and children will come to learn more naturally and be invigorated by the process. This will result in lower dropout rates and a greater love for learning. A child who loves school is simply in receipt of a lesson plan that specifically addresses the way in which he or she is wired.

At age twelve to sixteen, puberty begins to influence hygiene and environmental maintenance. Some kids will clearly become messier, and others are more neurotic in their need to present from a place of perfection. This issue of refinement and the variation thereof is discussed at length in chapter nine, using the analogy of ore. Are you gold, silver, copper, or a combination of two or more? We call this interval "the Alchemical Revelation," in that being able to identify one's alchemy or distinct level of refinement can and will determine their network of friends and boundaries of tolerance. Understanding alchemy defuses a great deal of misunderstandings between parents and children, employers and employees, and committees or countries in conflict. However, in today's world, without a clear understanding of alchemy, man is misjudged and persecuted daily. In most cases it feeds the fire that started the war.

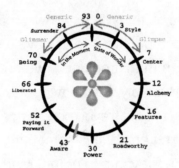

Age sixteen to twenty-one is the most reckless interval in our life, simply because the vehicle that we regard as our physical body has difficulty in determining who or what should drive it. Some individuals are driven by order and referred to as "control freaks." However, this is a misunderstanding, for without being able to create order, they cannot move forward. In truly loving them, we create opportunities for them to create order and control. Other people are motivated by creating protection, and this is best exemplified by those individuals who continue to petition for crosswalks, new laws, and streetlights. Essentially, there are many passengers in our vehicle, all of whom are competing for the driver's seat. Understanding what motivates and drives a sixteen-year-old can provide valuable insight when it comes to designing a career path that they can fully embrace.

Age twenty-one to thirty is when we reach maturity from a physical growth perspective. We achieve a state of full bloom at twenty-one, and from that point on, we are decidedly an adult by society. Unfortunately, just leaving the showroom floor for parts unknown, with little travel experience, hardly qualifies us for adulthood. Being an adult is something that is not naturally closely achievable for years to come. Man must weather "The Storm" before he can claim himself as an adult. Those who know that a storm lies ahead will prepare for it and sail through, while others may feel extremely broadsided and may not survive it. This is one of the great advantages of understanding The Cycle of Life™. It offers natural foresight and this presents an opportunity to truly be conscious in making choices that may impact your future.

Age thirty to forty-three is a very full interval. It is a segmented interval, because it is the most "inner life" transforming, where all other intervals are noticeably "outer" or physically evident. From thirty to thirty-four, we are experiencing tremendous fulfillment and self-indulgence. Some are getting married, climbing the corporate ladder, going back to school, buying houses, starting businesses, or having babies and deciding to stay home. It is a time when we see ourselves as special and significant. We call this the "Power Phase," simply because we have so much going for us, in that we are somewhat roadworthy, have about 55k on the odometer, not too many dings, and are extremely marketable. Then, as if in the blink of an eye, we wake up one morning uncomfortable and slightly dissatisfied with our current state of existence. This marks the beginning of something more than the result of a poor night's sleep or the previous day's discouraging circumstances ruminating through our thoughts. It's as if we were enveloped during our sleep by a thin veil of permeable Saran Wrap overnight. A subtle sensation of suffocation, claustrophobia, or tension begins to accompany our daily thoughts, and discontentment begins to manifest. The grass starts looking greener on the other side, and our current plans and aspirations take on a more lackluster appeal. Just for a minute imagine yourself a caterpillar at age zero, strolling through each interval until age thirty-four, and then all of a sudden, your journey suddenly ceases, leaving Mother Nature to cover you in her own blanket of protection so that you can emerge completely renewed on the other side at forty-three. We call this "Midlife Transformation" or rather "The Storm." Note the accent on the Cycle of Life™ graphic depicting age thirty-nine. This marks the *eye of the hurricane,* and for a moment there is a calm. It is during this interval that marriages fail; careers vanish; family members die; addictions manifest, escalate, or find healing; and a new sense of self emerges. No one is exempt from this interval. Everyone passes through it, some more easily than others.

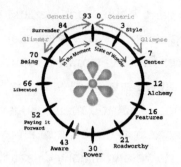

Age forty-three to fifty-two is a wonderful coming of age. It marks the beginning of adulthood. Where age twenty-one highlights physical maturity, adulthood is something that requires a history of experience in making conscious life decisions. You have weathered the storm and emerged a butterfly, sensing that a completely different life lies ahead. An opportunity to pursue a whole new outlook on life presents itself, and your perception of reality, purpose, and love hold a greater significance. Reasonability and a recognition of one's mortality becomes the focus of this interval. The need to gather more information, indulge in meaningful experiences, and take better care of your body becomes a priority. Gyms and fitness centers are filled with individuals from this demographic, trying to make up for lost time.

Age fifty-two to sixty-six brings with it personal forgiveness and understanding. All that we have collected over the past thirty years becomes fuel for the gift we are to leave behind as we begin to pay it forward. We are comfortable in our own skin, and for many of us, in spite of our vanity, we admit our age for the first time, feeling worthy of the respect it commands. There is a proud survivalist that shines through our smile and a need to let others know that each phase of life is glorious and deserves to be embraced fully.

It is not until age sixty-six that we experience liberation, a freedom from responsibility to this lifetime. It is a time that offers us an opportunity to try something new and fun. Many people choose to travel, take up piano playing, or paint landscapes. In today's world of health-consciousness, many are vibrant, active, and eager to dance, sing, and join organizations that celebrate life. These are the Golden Years, and can last from sixty-six to seventy or seventy-five, depending on the individual's state of health as they enter the interval.

At age seventy to seventy-five, the grandparent's or great-grandparent's wisdom prevails. Our motherboards are getting full, and maintaining lists becomes very important, so as not overload ourselves with trying to remember newly assigned tasks. Much is archived in the files of our physicality by this time, and nature will delete that which is most current, just like our computer's e-mail inbox when it reaches a high-water mark. It's important we learn how to discard that which is not important, so as to extend and improve the quality of our life. We don't want to crash our hard drive prematurely by trying to store when there is no room. Brain-fitness exercises like juggling and crossword puzzles keep our brain in shape but have little to do with its capacity for storage. Nature is simply taking its course as Father Time chronicles the fading of our physical presence.

From seventy-five to eighty-four, we hold dear the memories of our life and gradually begin to surrender all that takes from us energetically. Forgiving and forgetting begin to come naturally, and with this occurrence, the onset of a natural "surrender" follows. The beautiful thing about being human is that each phase of life holds a place for understanding. It is in this phase that we may struggle to reach acceptance as we are asked to prepare incrementally to release ourselves from the physicality that once held us to the earth. This is where we often see disease occur. The tug of war and the desire to thrive come face to face with a new order of divine purpose. The reality being, if you don't learn how to forgive, forget, and surrender early on, Mother Nature and Father Time will assist you in the end.

Age eighty-four to ninety-three is laced with spillage from the previous interval, if we are fortunate to have lived this long. Of course, there are those who live longer. Case in point, there was a woman who lived to be 106 years old. She was able to surround herself with clarity, comforts, and joy for most of her mature life. Her world was rarely challenged by the pollutants of life. Hardship and struggle were not in her life's plan, thus the wear and tear upon her vehicle was minimal as she entered this interval. She always ate right, got plenty of rest, exercised, and bought a new Easter bonnet every year. Unfortunately, today our water is polluted, our skies are filled with smog, and Mother Earth is asking repeatedly that we clean up our act. The words we share with one another are often damaging, and the messages sent through the media are riddled with toxicity that sprays its viral threat upon us daily like showers of soot. And often we cry out, feeling slimed, lost, and alone, for Mother Nature to bathe the windows of our soul so that we may see the truth of who we are. With The Knowledge of Y.O.U.®, you gain *your own understanding* before your energy centers return to that same state of the two you originally came in with. Like the infant arriving, man leaves in a similar generic state, requiring only three things: to be fed, to be changed, and to be loved.

Chapter Six

The Interval

Experiencing the Nature of Change
The most transformative time in your adult life.

"**T**he Interval" is an interesting topic of discussion. Formerly referred to over the ages as "the midlife crisis," "the frantic forties," "the transition," and "the red sports car," this phase of life continues to rear its ugly little head even when we spend thousands of dollars trying to become aware so that we may be spared the uncertainty that manifests in our chattering mind during this time. The truth is, it starts at age thirty-four and ends at forty-three, just like clockwork. Periodically, we may experience a slightly longer or shorter version, just like in pregnancy but the reality is, Mother Nature is in charge when it comes to The Interval. The only control that you have is in developing an understanding of it. And the good news is, if you don't develop an understanding of it, life will wake you up anyway once it passes. It is a gestation period. Whether you liken it to a caterpillar gradually experiencing greater degrees of confinement in a cocoon winding tighter as time progresses or carrying a fetus until such time as you experience the labor of birth, both reference becoming more uncomfortable as the end of your new beginning nears.

One of the injustices that man has imposed upon himself since first beginning to speak is the notion that he or she is an adult at or around twenty-one. The reality is, he or she is simply mature, in perfect bloom, or has reached full term and can be declared brand new, fully assembled, and roadworthy. In reality, one is not an adult and really does not *know himself.* "Adult" implies that he is ready, well-equipped to make intelligent choices while existing in an ignorant world. This is like trying to see clearly underwater in a muddy lake. Intelligence requires self-knowledge beyond likes and dislikes. If one enters The Interval slimed by life, it is likely that a great deal of disillusionment, hardship, and even self-destruction will take place. It's important that one try to remain clear-headed during this time. Unfortunately, in today's world, a large percentage of marriages fall apart during this time and children are left to suffer the effects of it all. Some remarry and others simply leave town, looking for something outside of themselves. Careers begin to have a lackluster appeal, and many often feel trapped by their own vain imaginings. Some feel sorry for themselves and others fear the sky is about to cave in on top of them. Nothing is as it seems during this time. Knowing that this is completely natural and that one's energy is likely to diminish, and life appears to be pedestrian, routine, and annoyingly repetitive, it's vital that intelligence prevail and you not throw the baby out with the bathwater.

The life you have created up until this point has been a cooperative effort, and even though it may feel like you are on the escalator to nowhere, you will arrive at a new destination and you will be pleasantly surprised. Back in the day when marriages lasted for fifty and sixty years, there was little to distract one from merely surviving. The bonds that formed in marriages and in the family institution were strong because family members saw and intermingled with each other daily. Prior to that era, women died during this interval because at age thirty-nine, which represents the eye of the hurricane, many would get pregnant for the last time. Their bodies could not take it, given the demands of a pioneer lifestyle. Consequently, the men who remained behind experienced change. And change is what this interval is all about. There is no other interval like it. It changes *you* forever and the people in your life. If you are wise and intelligent enough to hang on to the baby while making efforts to clean the water, then that which lies on other side will be paradise. If you choose to throw the baby out, you will be faced with loneliness, intermittent friendships, hidden guilt, and having to re-invent yourself. It's a very selfish time, and most of us just don't know how to handle it. The voices in our head are louder than usual and the discontentment and sensitivity to all that was once familiar (people we loved, places we call home, and once-favorite pastimes) all become close to intolerable. We are not feeling like the same person. We are essentially a trapped caterpillar inside an ill-fitting sleeping bag.

In spite of the fact that it may feel like suffocating or being held prisoner in our world, it's vital we not discard anything or anyone during this time. Infidelity and harebrained schemes will pound upon your door. Should you decide to open the door, there will be consequences that will impact every moment of your existence from that point on. Total peace becomes a long way off, and self-discovery introduces new, painful realities of life that otherwise would never have come about. As age forty commences, our thought processes become more refined, providing we haven't fallen prey to drugs or alcohol, trying to sedate the voices in our head. This means common sense begins to whisper in our ear as a new sense of reality begins to manifest. New opportunities that never before seemed possible show up in your life, and eventually, life as you know it is changing rapidly.

At age forty-two, you get to catch your breath, rest, recover, and heal from the trauma that was imposed *naturally* upon you during this time. It is a birthing process. This survival brings about a great gift. This gift is *adulthood.* It is not until we reach forty-three that we can truly call ourselves an adult. In fact, many of us stay in denial right up until our forty-third birthday. But just like the sun rising, so does our welcoming of adulthood as we begin to viscerally understand that we only have one body and one life, and that making history with someone requires total commitment. In absolute *truth,* you wake up to a new *you* and become as aware as you are clean. If you are in this interval, know that it is only temporary. Do not discard, dismiss, or degrade anyone or anything during this time. Stay calm, stay clear, and stay true to yourself in knowing that change is taking place and you are to do nothing but lie still in the cocoon until such time as Mother Nature urges you to emerge and fly. Remember, it is not a straightjacket but just another womb. Those who feel confined and emerge prematurely suffer greatly in the days that follow. Don't fight it or blame others for your discontent. You have to fake it till you make it. I call it the bridge of pretending.

The human being is an interesting creature. It operates in three modes: intelligent, ignorant, and pretend. When it takes good care of itself, it exhibits signs of intelligence, and when self-maintenance is overlooked, it begins to exhibit symptoms of ignorance. Unfortunately, we live in a fairly toxic world, even in the most remote, pristine areas of human existence. Consequently, the ability to maintain an intelligent presentation is almost impossible; thus, we have created a third method of performance called *pretending*. We do this to keep moving forward and to manage our physical energy wisely. We are in the pretend mode every time we pretend we like something, when in truth we don't. How many times have you pretended to enjoy a meal, an activity, or an event, when in fact in you didn't care for any of it? The reasons for not being honest are multi-faceted, but truthfully it boils down to remaining energy efficient. Very few people are privileged to live in a world of constant intelligence, simply because ignorance permeates every fiber of our environment. Words of ignorance are often woven with threads of disease and ill intent. We find ourselves manipulative, intimidating, negligent, and self-absorbed almost daily. Pretending is choosing the middle road, mediocrity, and being average in a world where few have respect for intelligence. Intelligence is not "being book smart." It is knowing how to stay clean in a dirty world. It's understanding the significance of bringing yourself to center daily and the role that meditation, taking long, quiet walks, and singing in the rain have to offer. Journaling, jogging, and making faces out of the clouds as you lie down on a blanket of grass are all methods of bathing oneself. We have to do those things that maintain the integrity of our being. It's a dirty world out there, and if you don't know how to dust yourself off regularly, you'll become a proponent of toxicity and contribute only disease to this lifetime. The Interval is when our immune system becomes most vulnerable in terms of making intelligent choices. It is very easy to subscribe to ignorance, simply because we no longer have a clear view. Mother Nature wants us to be still and discover ourselves, but society and family demand our presence as usual. This requires that we stand strong in our mode of pretend until such time as nature allows us to proceed with a more enlightened understanding of life and how it really works.

Life in this interval has you restless, unhappy, and making excuses for why things are no longer satisfying. If you feel trapped and stifled by the very lifestyle you have helped to co-create, then you must begin to seek ways to calm your anxiety and distract your thoughts. Tell yourself, "This is only temporary" and "I can choose to love and be happy today" or "I can choose to embrace those who love me deeply." Be in the moment. Live only for today and not a minute longer. Do not look at tomorrow for a single second and do not look over the fence at how much greener your neighbor's grass is in comparison to yours. Your ability to judge during this time is veiled by nature's cocoon. Use this time to explore and expand your own inner understanding of what you are about to become and how you can be the best you can be. Should you take this advice, the rewards that come on the other side of this interval are many and most importantly offer a history of commitment and love. Be strong enough to endure the insanity of this growth period. Growing pains make us incredibly uncomfortable in our own skin but breed tremendous strength of character.

Don't give up the history you have created with another; you lose a part of yourself when you make this choice. Stay whole, stay true. Focus on being love rather than being in love. Love is the oxygen of life. It will keep you in check during this very natural and temporary time of life. There's a lot to be said for "this too shall pass," because it is absolutely *true!*

The following case studies exemplify the trials and tribulations that accompany this interval. In each scenario, pay special attention to choices and outcomes.

When Dreams Don't Come True

Ann's husband had been killed in a motorcycle accident. At age forty-six, she was left alone to parent their two sons, ages twelve and fourteen. This was *not* in her plan. She was heartbroken and angry. Outbursts of laughter and tears simultaneously expressed themselves. She cried out, "Now what?" Her desire to speak and come to a place of peace and understanding had become her mission of the moment.

Ann relayed to me that she and Steve had met when she was thirty and Steve was twenty-five. At that time in her life, Ann had just finished her bridesmaid duties for the fifth roommate that year! Always the bridesmaid, never the bride, she felt her biological clock ticking away. Aside from this natural need to be a wife and mother, she was enjoying life. She had a great job and wonderful friends. This was enhanced by involvement with her church singles group and related fun activities. Oftentimes she played the guitar and sang at group events. One evening, while she was performing at the Glory Café, Steve showed up to manage the sound board. Ann had known Steve through church, but he had disappeared from the scene months ago, as he was navigating his own relationship roller coaster. They hit it off instantly. He was cute, strong, smart, athletic, and available. After a brief courtship, they made their relationship exclusive. Two months later, they were married. Both were excited to be married and ready to begin a family. In their current state of love, the world was a wonderful place!

They began their new life laughing over Ann's dinner menu of quesadillas and popcorn. Ann had a good-paying job, which allowed Steve an opportunity to climb his own corporate ladder. Eight months after the wedding, Ann was pregnant with their first child. All was well and life was good. When their first son arrived, like many infants, he had colic and sleep was slim. Both Steve and Ann had full-time jobs, and the baby went to daycare. Ann would cry daily as she dropped him off, longing to be an "at-home" mom. The tension between the two of them rose, and bickering became the norm.

Along came baby number two. Ann was now thirty-four. She was disenchanted with the corporate world and longed to raise her family instead of leaving her two sons with the sitter for nine hours a day. She would come home, cook dinner, and bathe the boys while Steve stood outside, chatting with the neighbors. Resentments were manifesting quickly. Steve was clueless, and she was angry and tired. Additionally, Steve was struggling with his own demons at work, which expressed themselves at home as anger and volatility. He was defensive and much like a volcano waiting to erupt. Morning arguments were a stimulant to him. He would be yelling at Ann as she backed down the driveway to take the kids to daycare. He once threw his coffee cup at the driver's side of the car, sending it shattering and crashing to the ground. Ann, protected by a layer of glass, watched as the veins bulged on his angry forehead. What had she gotten herself into? How could she leave? Where would she go? The rest of the Ann's day was spent in a "fight hangover," while Steve seemed invigorated.

As the kids grew, Ann and Steve would cycle through fights, fear, and frustration, shutting down to one another and making up again. Ann didn't think she could leave him for verbal abuse. Yes, he was violent toward her, but he never hit her. At times she would provoke, wanting to be struck so she could leave. Holes were punched in walls, windows were broken by slamming doors, arms were bruised by angry holds. Their oldest son would hide in his room, while the youngest would cry to distract their angry outbursts.

Ann desperately wanted loving attention and to get her world in order. Steve felt as though Ann was too controlling. He loved to accomplish big projects and to initiate the change necessary to make projects come to fruition. When anything got in his way, he would become loud, intimidating, and volatile.

At last, Ann was able to leave her corporate job to stay at home. At first, she was delighted. But soon thereafter, she was depressed. Isn't this what she had been longing for? Wasn't this her loving duty? She was no longer in control of her life or recognized by anyone for anything. Nothing gave her peace of mind. She was adrift amid a sea of diapers, dinners, and mental downtime.

Steve would become particularly hostile when he drank. He began to turn his rage upon their three-year-old son, berating him with angry words. Steve had been abused as a child, and the cycle was continuing. Ann frequently ran interference. This was definitely *not* what she had signed up for. When Steve went on his bike rides, she would pray that if he got hit by a car, he would die. During this time, divorce attorneys were retained and angry incidents were documented, but nothing was ever filed or served.

Things began to calm down when Steve was promoted and the family relocated from Colorado to California. Damaging arguments still arose, but less frequently. Everyone was thrilled, as this was Steve's long-awaited career opportunity. Ann welcomed their change of environment because she had grown up in California and had a support system there.

Several years passed and Ann was beginning to distance herself from The Interval. Steve and Ann decided it was okay to "agree to disagree" on certain matters, rather than fight over who was right. Whenever something went amiss, Ann would jokingly take the blame to defuse the wick on the stick of dynamite. Steve was held in high regard by his colleagues, and his improved self-esteem made him a much happier soul. Ann found her "voice" and figured out how to communicate with Steve in a more effective manner. Steve coached baseball and soccer. He managed their oldest son's band. Life became much more manageable, and Ann could see Steve growing into the man she had always dreamt of. Both would take daily walks together to download the day's activities. They began to love again and to share new hope for the future. At this time,

Steve was a month shy of forty-one years old, and it seemed as though he was coming into a place of calm confidence. Shortly thereafter, Steve was struck by a car. The motorist had turned left in front of him while he was on his motorcycle, less than five miles from home. He died on the scene. A police officer stood at Ann's door, informing her of her loss. Now she was left to pick up the pieces and try to catch up with herself as she had been launched into a new and unfamiliar reality.

Ann's story is not an uncommon one, particularly in this tumultuous time of life between the ages of thirty-four and forty-three. Ann longed to get married only to find that once in, she wanted out. She ached for the fulfillment of motherhood and cried when she dropped her children off at daycare. When she finally realized her dream of being an "at-home" mom, she ended up depressed and lonely. This is a time of highs and lows, expectations and disappointments, as well as great victories.

In hindsight, Ann wished she had been better equipped to manage these changes and to manage her emotions during this time. She wished she had known how to love and support Steve, as reviewed in chapter four. She wished she had known how to bathe her husband and children so the family unit could thrive. She wished she had truly known her role as a woman and how vitally important that role is in today's world. She wished she had known what fueled Steve and how she could have supported him, thus encouraging better behavior.

Ann and I had the opportunity to spend many sessions discussing these topics and how The Ultimate Life Tool® assessment is vitally important in bringing health to the individual and the family unit. Ann became so excited about the depth and breadth of this knowledge that she became a practitioner with the Y.O.U. Consulting Group. She is now a sought-after speaker and advisor.

Sailing Single through the Storm

As mentioned in the case study above, the interval between the ages of thirty-four and forty-three can be very rocky indeed. I have found that sailing through this interval single, while still bumpy, can be a much smoother ride. While those who are sailing single may disagree with me, there is much less collateral damage traversing life as a single as compared to the muck some are dragged through while married with children. Given the right attitude, this can be a great ride!

Let's take a look at Matt. Matt was on top of the world at age thirty. He was living in Chicago and was a professional sports agent. He loved his job. He got to represent the best of the best to the who's who in sports. He was handsome and in good shape, which provided him an array of female companions. He chose his own hours, worked hard, and played even harder. At age thirty-four, Matt was grateful for this lifestyle, yet he began to feel lonely and unfulfilled. All of a sudden, he found himself asking, "Is this all there is?" Although beautiful women passed through his life, as though moving through a turnstile, he longed for the stability that a committed, monogamous relationship had to offer.

He had a friend who lived in Beverly Hills, California. Matt figured a change of scenery would be good for him. So he loaded up his truck, albeit a Cadillac Escalade, and drove to Beverly Hills. He had enough money to live for a couple of months before deciding whether or not to relocate. Matt immediately fell in with a similar crowd and began enjoying the California lifestyle, fine dining and parties with young, hip stars. Keeping up with the trend, he joined a spiritual center to address his need to feel connected and grounded. He was very excited by the philosophy and personal development classes offered through the center. This was a new experience for him.

While attending a class at the center, he became acquainted with a record producer. Matt had a degree in business with a minor in music, so their discussions flowed freely. Matt was offered a fabulous job. He was grateful for the ease with which this transpired. This meant his days as a sports agent could be put to rest and he could stay in California. His new career enabled him to meet many lovely women. Some were in his life longer than others, but he still had not found "the one" for him. While working in California, Matt received word that his father had been diagnosed with colon cancer. Matt's mother had died some years prior, and his siblings did not have the flexibility to manage the care associated with a disease of this magnitude. Being the chosen one, Matt quickly flew to New York to see his father through surgery, recovery, and if necessary, chemotherapy. His employer praised him for his noble and selfless effort and promised him a job upon his return.

While taking care of his father and visiting him in the hospital, Matt met a beautiful young nurse and fell head over heels in love. He was sure he had met "the one," and in short order asked her to marry him. Unfortunately, his certainty was not shared by her. She expressed concern about being ready for marriage. Matt was clearly a wonderful person worthy of her love, but there were many unanswered questions. Where would they live? Did he want children? Was he capable of supporting them financially? When these questions were not answered to her satisfaction, she pulled a disappearing act. Matt was devastated. He began to question himself and was consumed with doubt. He was thirty-seven and living with his ailing father. He had only a few friends in a new city and he was heartbroken.

This was Matt's state of mind when he called my office. He had found The Ultimate Life Tool® on the Internet, taken the test, and requested further advisement to relieve him of his anxiety. Here was an accomplished, well-educated man adrift without a compass. We discussed the fact that he was in The Interval. Furthermore, his results indicated that he had a positive disposition and a gregarious nature. His wide range of tolerance for various levels of refinement made him flexible and easy to get along with. He had great monetary discretion and understood the ebb and flow of cash. He was very compassionate, and helping others fueled his being. I shared the characteristics of the women who would best suit him and with whom he could connect. We confirmed that he liked to live in warm environments, close to the water. After hearing all of this, it was as if Matt had been thrown a lifeline. He quickly was able to adjust his attitude, correct his course, and make decisions in alignment with his nature.

Matt continues to check in regularly by phone. His father is doing well, and Matt is back on the West Coast. He has returned to his previous job and is now married to a wonderful woman. Both he and his wife take The Ultimate Life Tool® online assessment twice a year, and we have fun catching up through phone consultations. Matt and his wife have a common language through The Ultimate Life Tool® technology. This helps them love and honor the unique beings that they are and embrace their differences. And, having survived The Interval with little to no collateral damage, made it possible for his current relationship to come in over a calm sea.

Chapter Seven

Seven Ways to See Others

What Natural Traits Reveal
Addressing how nature repeats itself and how it specifically shows up
visually in each individual on the planet. Holding up the mirror to yourself
and knowing what your physical appearance has to say about you, clothed
or otherwise.

*R*emember back in chapter one, where the questions
were posed about the cactus and the pine tree? What
we do know just by looking at a cactus and a pine tree is that
the former doesn't produce nearly as much shade as the latter.
We also know that if we took a cactus from the hot, dry climate
in which it thrives and replanted it in a cold, wet climate, it
would not survive. At the same time, you don't see many pine
trees in the desert, do you? Let's take a look at dogs. We know
that a pit bull naturally has a more aggressive tendency than a
golden retriever and this makes this animal far more attractive
in protecting people and environments. On the other hand, the
approachable nature of the golden retriever ensures us that it
is likely the weaker choice in selecting a guard dog candidate.
Are you starting to get the picture? We can look at most things
found in nature and know what to expect from them in terms
of potential, yet when human beings look at each other they
often have no idea *what* they are looking at. We are the only

species on the planet that cannot see itself. Because of this, people often place their own expectations on others, and that's when relationships start to break down. Worse yet, they are often misled by a person's socially influenced false dress and attitude. There's a lot of "you should do this and you should do that" out there. The Knowledge of Y.O.U.® and The Ultimate Life Tool® technology teaches each one of us how to *see* ourselves and others for the unique individuals that we are.

Learning how to *see* each other will ultimately allow individuals to eliminate misconceptions they may have about themselves and misconceptions they may have about others, so that they can literally approach each relationship in every area of life with understanding, non-judgment, and complete acceptance. That's a pretty powerful statement, isn't it? What The Knowledge of Y.O.U.® and The Ultimate Life Tool® technology reveal to us is the perfection of our individual unique design. Obviously, each one of us is uniquely different. Much like the many different cars in a parking lot, we each have a unique physical appearance, special capabilities, and our own way of experiencing life. Each one of us is also perfectly designed, yet for many people, this perfection has become distorted. Many people travel through life, operating from a mode of what others believe is best for them or from a place where others feel they should be spending their time and energy, rather than from a place that naturally suits them as the one-of-a-kind individuals that they are.

Would you take a Maserati off-roading in the desert? Probably not, but a Jeep would do quite well. The same is true for human beings. The Ultimate Life Tool® technology gives each one of us our very own operating manual—for the very vehicle that is you. Having this operating manual will give you the ability to make conscious decisions about what you do and how you do it. Some of you are extremely perceptive and can process information at lightning speed. Some of you can absorb volumes of information and have easy access to retrieving it. Some of you are designed to have chiseled bodies. Some of you are designed to have fuller figures. Some of you are extremely energetic. Some of you actually need to take a nap every day to rejuvenate yourself. Some of you are designed to be performers or spokespeople. Some of you are designed to work behind the scenes. Yet again, each one of you is perfectly designed, and understanding your unique design through The Knowledge of Y.O.U.® and The Ultimate Life Tool® technology will allow you put your energy in to honoring that design, rather than trying to change it or trying to fit into something that just will not work for you.

How physical law, specifically the law of gravity, shows up in each one of us is revealed through our physicality. This is an important factor to consider when understanding what to expect from yourself, as well as another, in terms of potential. What if you took a bowling ball and a feather and dropped them both at the same time from the top of a ten-story building? We obviously can deduce that the bowling ball will fall to the ground first. But consider the feather, it may take a very long time to reach the ground, and depending upon the breeze, may never reach it. Like the bowling ball, some people are physically more grounded. They naturally show up with more mass, and as you will see later in this chapter, it is imperative that they honor this trait. Others may appear "light as a feather"; they are physically lighter and have a fragility about them that needs to be recognized and honored as well. Still others lie somewhere in between. This is the law of gravity revealing itself in human beings, and understanding this law helps us to see why it is that people need to be doing certain things from a gravitational perspective.

Just like any traditional archetype, one can look at the gravity of human beings as archetypical in nature. And in observing nature, we have to honor the fundamentals of mathematics, in that there are seven wonders of the world, seven days of the week, seven continents, seven colors in the rainbow, seven bodily functions, and so on and so on. Similarly, The Knowledge of Y.O.U.® provides us with seven ways of seeing our physicality. They show up as seven spokes on the wheel of life, as diagrammed below.

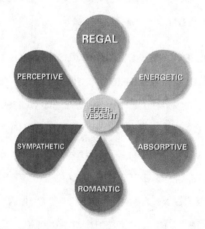

In observing these seven ways of seeing our physicality, it is important to realize that each one of us is comprised of all seven spokes, yet typically only three or four of these spokes are most obvious or prominent. This means they are on our desktop; one can physically see the traits that reveal individual potential. Understanding what those specific traits are within each spoke allows one to identify potential in oneself and another simply by looking.

When you look at yourself in the mirror, what are the most obvious physical traits that you notice? What is your skin tone for your ethnicity—is it dark, medium, or light? Consider your body type; are you muscular or curvaceous or do you have a thick waist? What is the shape of your face? Is it oval, square, or round? Do you have pointed facial features or are they more chiseled? Is your hair thick or thin; is it dark or light? What is your eye color, and do your eyes have a sparkle to them?

All of these things you can observe about yourself and others at first glance. They are the physical traits we came into this world with, and they lie in the objective obvious. They cannot be changed (unless surgically altered) and they make us the unique individuals that we are.

In addition to specific physical traits, each of the seven spokes also possesses specific natural traits or dispositions. So let's examine what each spoke looks like. The first order of business lies with describing a very majestic, regal presentation. We see this in nature when we look at a mountain or a redwood tree, or even when we look at animals such as a giraffe or a Clydesdale. They all have a commanding presence about them. They are all physically tall. This presentation means something, in that they all have the ability to take on an aerial perspective in their environment. When this spoke shows up in the obvious in human beings (meaning we can notice it at first glance), these individuals will be physically tall or appear taller than they actually are. Again, they have a presence about them that gives them the ability to see the big picture in most circumstances and the ability to fashion solutions for the benefit of the whole. Because of their physical presentation, they are able to naturally maintain a regal approach to their environment and those residing in it. This feels benevolent at times, and it is believable because it comes naturally. It is the midpoint of masculinity and individuals, males or females, with this prominent spoke are quite simply natural born leaders and decision-makers.

The next spoke presents itself as extremely energetic with a very sturdy powerhouse build. Individuals with this prominent spoke are easily identified by their chiseled facial features or square jaw line. Along with their pronounced energetic nature comes an aggressive "in-your-face" approach to life that tends to be confrontational in nature. Going back to the pit bull example, this particular spoke is very prominent in this animal. When this spoke shows up in human beings, they present with all of the above qualities, along with an enthusiasm and passion that has them believing strongly in truth and justice. These individuals are filled with integrity, and they thrive on taking action, often taking the quickest route between A and B to get the job done. They are the knights and crusaders of society.

The earlier example about the bowling ball directly relates to the next spoke on the Wheel of Life. From a gravitational perspective, this spoke is very grounded. In order for it to maintain this state of reliability, it physically has more mass. Individuals with this prominent spoke tend to be more round and full through the middle. These individuals have the capacity to absorb vast amounts of information that they archive and retrieve at will. Because of this, it is actually imperative that they do not fall prey to societal standards encouraging them to appear thinner than they are. They will literally lose vital energy. How sad would it be to see a malnourished elephant, a creature that is worshipped and revered by many! Yet we as humans often misjudge our human counterpart's magnificence, disallowing opportunities for them to share their gifts. Many have simply adopted an invalid socially imposed perception of weight or gravitational significance. Everyone and everything that is three-dimensional has a little "elephant" in them, some much more than others. Libraries are another example, and of course there is the state of Texas. Both possess great memories and obviously "never forget." This particular spoke is passive and positive and naturally presents itself as extremely happy, joyful, and generous. These individuals tend to be the heart of the party, and because of their absorptive nature, their understanding of life is deep, as opposed to being superficial.

This next spoke is easily identified by looking at one's physicality as it relates to the shape of their bodies. Individuals with this prominent spoke tend to have oddly proportioned bodies, meaning not of the majority. They can have long legs or a high waist, or vice versa; sometimes they will have a sloping chin or sloping shoulders and round or oval faces. This spoke is more reclusive in nature. These individuals revel in silence and serenity and have an easy ability to be still and go inward for relaxation purposes. They also tend to have a great desire for an intimate rapport with their surroundings. This is the midpoint of femininity, and people with this prominent spoke are very passive, gentle, and romantic. Many "gentlemen" have a strong presence in this spoke. Unlike the energetic spoke that is confrontational, this presentation is non-confrontational, very loyal, and devoted. These individuals are extremely reliable, and though they work most effectively behind the scenes, many will work long hours, get the job done, and do it well.

The most obvious physical trait we see when we look at this next spoke is a thick head of hair and/or an above average amount of hair on other parts of the body, such as the face, arms, legs and back. When this spoke is prominent in an individual, it is imperative that they make sure to budget their energy wisely. They have a very sympathetic and nurturing presentation that needs to rejuvenate itself daily in order to stay on top of its game. It is vital for an individual with this spoke to take a reprieve between 2 and 4 PM every day. Get some fresh air, take a catnap, or listen to some soothing music for twenty minutes to disconnect and recharge. They will find they have more energy as a result of forfeiting this daily time. Because this spoke is passive and positive in nature, it this sends a signal that everything is going to be okay. Its very laid-back, relaxed nature also gives one the gift of putting things off till tomorrow without worry; at times one may even require some prodding to get things done. At the same time, people feel the genuine presentation of care and concern displayed toward others, and it allows an individual with this prominent spoke to produce a response of acceptance in most any situation. Someone with this prominent spoke naturally has the ability to make friends and influence people.

One of the most obvious physical traits we notice when we look at what is revealed through the next spoke is narrow, pointed facial features. Individuals with this prominent spoke also have smaller, dark eyes. This spoke is highly perceptive, meaning individuals can process information at lightning speed. However, because they are active and negative in nature, they will be more covert in their approach and look at what is not working first when addressing a situation or environment. Individuals with this prominent spoke can be cunning, mysterious, and even a little sneaky at times. This is not ill intended; they simply do not feel the need to reveal everything unless it is absolutely necessary. Even though it may feel like a hidden agenda to some, they don't waste precious energy sharing plans with those who cannot carry them out or contribute to the focus of their manifestation. The individual with this prominent spoke is very curious and likes to explore and investigate, which can be attractive and alluring for interested parties.

The final spoke on the Wheel of Life can be instantly identified simply by looking at a person's eyes. Individuals with this prominent spoke have eyes that sparkle! Oftentimes it's the first thing you notice about them, and frequently it is attached to a smile. They are extremely effervescent in nature and carry an optimistic view of reality. From a gravitational perspective, they have a fragility about them. The more pronounced this spoke appears in an individual, the more one needs to pay attention to this fragility. Unlike the grounded bowling ball, this spoke is like the feather. It has to expend a large amount of energy to stay on the ground. Individuals with prominence in this spoke are extremely kind and considerate. This genuine, accepting nature allows for an inviting presence that makes this individual very approachable in business and in life. It also gives them a comfortable ease when presenting themselves to the world. They cultivate many interests and tend to develop an understanding from that of an observer or through the eyes of wonder, as seen in a young child. This spoke is active and positive in nature, and it will address what *is* working first in an environment or situation. This positive approach, coupled with a radiant nature, allows an individual to simply "light up a room."

"Seeing is believing" and "appearances are not deceiving"— these are nature's clues to understanding human nature. We subscribe to the same laws of nature as plants and animals. We did not show up in these bodies by accident. There is a purpose riding on us. So, the next time you look at a family member, a friend, a client, a co-worker, or even yourself, consider what you are looking at rather than who you are looking at. Until we learn how to see each other and honor every individual unique design, we will continue to place our own expectations on others, and this will continue to provide fuel for relationship breakdown. We each have an operating manual that is specific and unique to each one of us.

We are not meant to be doing the same things the same way as each other. The Knowledge of Y.O.U.® and The Ultimate Life Tool® technology teach us how to reach our potential effortlessly and give us input so that we can make quality decisions based on our own unique design.

The CUTE Syndrome

Sidney pounded my desk with her fist. "I'm never taken seriously! I am forty-two years old and well educated, and when I stand in a room pitching a brilliant screenplay, I can see their eyes rolling like I am a goof—and then I get asked out to lunch!"

Sidney is a visionary and a fabulous author and screenwriter. Her brilliance affords her the ability to see the world "outside of the box," which makes her screenplays innovative and exciting. Unfortunately, she is not being received respectfully by her peers. She is blonde with big blue eyes that sparkle, has a bright and infectious smile, and is quite thin with a fragile appearance. Added to this delightful package is a small, childlike voice, a cross Sydney has had to bear her entire life. Phone solicitors would often call and ask if they could speak with her mother. She would retort, "I *am* the mother!" And to make matters worse, whenever she goes to her local coffeehouse, the barista always greets her with a, "Good morning, sweetie!" To most, all of these qualities would seem a wonderful asset. However, sporting the "cute syndrome" while establishing credibility does not fuel one's success. The telling moment comes every time she stands before her peers in a boardroom pitching one of her brilliant ideas, only to be dismissed as a cute, dumb blonde not worth their time or consideration.

Using The Ultimate Life Tool®, I was able to help Sidney see the potential that her physical appearance provided to her professional pursuit. I explained that the value of her natural traits was best expressed in her ability to see life through the eyes of wonder. Her visionary-like perception and rationale afforded her the ability to create something new and wonderful for mankind to experience. Her physicality indicated that she was a wise one with a young heart that could tap into the imagination at will. Furthermore, we examined her perfection in depth and came up with a strategy that permitted her to stand before her peers in a more defined and purposeful manner. To support her physical presence, I suggested Sidney partner with someone who had a majestic presence. This would serve as a complement to her effervescence and offer a better balance to her presentations. She was to choose someone with a deeper voice and a more commanding appearance; someone who is noticed and respected the moment they walk through the door. This person would be her voice in setting her up for success.

This suggestion proved to be a winning proposition for all parties. Because of the understanding derived from The Ultimate Life Tool®, Sidney now gets to see her gifts become a reality that others are able to experience and enjoy.

Resourcing Andrea

Andrea came to see me as a result of repeated confrontational experiences in the workplace. She was the director of human resources for a well-known publication and, as part of the executive team, sat in on most strategizing meetings. She was highly qualified and able to attract the best of the best to the magazine. Andrea got along quite well with her male counterparts. However, problems arose when her very direct manner of communicating consistently cut people to the quick. She began to be alienated from all outside work activities, and complaints were submitted to the president on a regular basis. Andrea would be blunt and forthright and then become apologetic about her delivery. This behavior started to undermine her authority. Even though she was aware of her not-so-well-received, very direct nature, she still felt it necessary to be the one to convey the information.

Prior to Andrea's addition to the executive team, The Y.O.U. Consulting Group had performed an executive review. The president was pleased with the value that Andrea brought to his organization, and he knew there was a workable solution by using the information highlighted in The Ultimate Life Tool®. I was contacted to sit with Andrea, to listen to her, and to then offer workable suggestions. I was able to make an initial visual assessment, and her report confirmed my observations.

When I looked at Andrea, I could see instantly that she was a crusader. This made her a valuable asset to the magazine, as she strongly believed in their mission and stood by the importance of their vision and culture. Honoring truth and justice was a prominent trait in Andrea; it was obvious that she had little tolerance for anyone or anything that did not fall into line. She pointed this out in a most "in-your-face" manner. Andrea naturally worked hard and was very loyal. She had the fine quality of perseverance, and took the most direct path between points A and B. If anyone thwarted her forward movement by way of an interruption in the flow of her day, she became resistant and curt in her responses.

Another aspect of her physicality was her stature. This sent a very commanding message that she possessed a very natural ability to hold court and assume responsibility. By nature, she was benevolent and had a panoramic perspective on life. She could see the big picture and made decisions for the benefit of all. Last but not least, she was highly perceptive and could process information very quickly. She was the first to see what was not working in a situation or environment. This worked well in her current position, because the executive team relied on her ability to see the weak spots and quickly shore them up.

I explained that the crusader in her was the aspect that people most respected. However, I suggested that when she found herself feeling irritated or intolerant, she take a deep breath before speaking or digging in her heels. It might be more beneficial to switch to her regal side and consider herself in the equation before cutting someone with her words. And it would be perfectly okay to join the ranks by openly sharing what she was hired to do and then create solutions to improve the situation. Andrea agreed with my assessment and suggestions. It restored her self-respect and grounded the value that her being brought to the organization.

I truly enjoyed my time with Andrea and suggested to both her and the president that she acquaint herself with our technology and possibly become a resident expert. Having a deeper understanding of The Knowledge of Y.O.U.® would continue to create confidence in her personal gifts as well as adding value to her role as director of human resources.

Chapter Eight

What Motivates You?

Knowing what naturally drives you
Knowing what drives YOU, your vehicle; how to manage the voices in your head.

*I*f our body is the vehicle transporting our spirit around in this lifetime, who is driving? Do they have a driver's license? Do they know where they are going and where to get gas? Probably not. If everyone knew this about themselves, this world would not be in the state of misunderstanding that it is today. In watching the daily news (not recommended), it's as if everyone has run out of gas, has no clue where they are going, and likely has no clue as to what kind of gas they require in order to move forward.

In nature, there exist twelve distinct behaviors that permeate and illustrate nuclear force. These same twelve physical demonstrations are as real as the months in a year and the hands on a clock. The only thing that sets them apart from their relationship with time is their relationship with human nature. When we witness a behavior, whether it is an expression of joy or a gust of wind, each has a beginning, middle, and end. Additionally, each has its high point and its low point.

Understanding the highs and lows of human nature leads to self-mastery.

Frequently we are faced with individuals who behave badly or demonstrate ignorance. What is it that happened to change them from an intelligent person to an ignorant one? We do not come in this way. Our body knows how to heal itself and we love quite naturally until such time as we fall prey to the toxicity of this lifetime. To best describe what happens, one must first know what good behavior looks like as it pertains to a *unique* individual. In fully conveying the mathematics of man, it is vital that each individual know what *naturally* motivates them. For some, it is creating order, and for others, it may be creating protection. There are even those who possess a feature or motivator that requires they initiate change. These individuals are great for cleaning house in a business culture or in their personal environment. Some can be equally as talented in refurbishing and flipping houses. Each of the twelve motivators resides in your vehicle like a minivan full of kids. However, some of us are small cars trying to stay on the road while managing a carload of chatterboxes. The Ultimate Life Tool® technology actually reveals how loud and crowded your car may be. When we get too loud, we are prone to crash. Knowing what naturally motivates you gives you an opportunity to stay clear, allowing intelligence to prevail.

As an observer, caring for others comes in understanding nuclear force. When a person whines, uses "I" a lot, panics, resists, intimidates, manipulates, deprives, digs in their heels, or attacks another, we are witnessing weak nuclear force via human expression. We call this ignorance in action.

Ignorance is like a red alert. It tells us that toxicity has consumed this person and now they are at risk to themselves and others. It is a cry for help, healthy fuel, or a car wash. The more toxic we are, the less likely we are able to *see* or even guess where we are going. It's like traveling down the road in a wet dust storm. If the windshield is covered in mud, not much good is likely to come from your day. When our children, bosses, or retail clerks snap and yell at us, we know they are headed for confusion. Coming from a place of weakness on a regular basis creates disease; not good. Toxicity usually first surfaces meeting the HALT criteria. If you catch yourself behaving poorly, ask yourself, "Am I hungry, angry, lonely, or tired?" If you can answer yes to one of these, you must take time to clean your "windshield" as soon as possible. There are many ways to do this. Because we each are unique, we may require our own special squeegee and solution. For some, it is curling up with a good book. For others, it may be a bubble bath or game of racquetball. Thanks to the ULT technology, trained YCG professionals know what works for every human on the planet. Everyone is intuitive ... *everyone!* IT, InTuition, serves as an oil filter. However, when that oil filter gets dirty from living in a toxic world, our drivers lose sight of where they are going. When someone tells me they are very intuitive, I often silently respond, "Yes, but are you intuiting ignorance or intelligence?"

Being able to *see* is knowing what kind of behavior is natural for another and what is not. Those with a compulsion for creating order are notoriously called controlling. However, if you knew that giving your loved one the opportunity to organize and create order fed them, oxygenated them, fueled them, and made them feel good, might you be more loving? *Love* embraces one's strong nuclear force and seeks opportunities for it to perform. This results in happiness for all concerned. It makes people feel *seen,* understood, respected, supported, and loved. To better understand what drives you, go online and take the online Ultimate Life Tool® test. Your seven-page report will give you a full explanation of how to stay on the road of life as it pertains specifically to *you.*

Life on the Other Side

When my client walked into my office, I was shocked! This handsome, rugged ex-marine had a black eye, bruises on his face, and his knuckles were cut. He winced as he sank into my couch, holding his ribs. It was obvious he had been in a fight. I thought he had grown past his angry outbursts. "Bruce, what happened this time? Are things between you and Mary all right?"

"Yeah, this had nothing to do with Mary. I got laid off of my construction job and I went to the bar to console myself with some drinks. I was angry! I didn't want to tell Mary I got laid off. We have been struggling financially. I just couldn't go home right away. Anyway, this guy got in my face and wouldn't back off. I decked him, and then I was jumped by his friends. We all got thrown into jail, and *that* is how Mary found out I got laid off. Now I have to appear in court for drunk and disorderly behavior. When will I ever learn?"

Bruce was twenty-two and had been in the Marine Corps for four years. He had served three tours of duty: one in

Afghanistan and two in Iraq. I was fortunate to be part of YCG's effort to assist our returning soldiers cope with their overseas experiences. The goal was to help them choose careers on "the outside" and develop strong relationships with their wives or husbands upon their return. Bruce had that military look. He had a strong, sturdy body, chiseled features, and a square jaw. His angry outbursts used to be directed toward his wife, Mary. Fortunately, those days were behind them. Apparently, he still had to suffer the consequences of his behavior.

One of Bruce's motivators is all about initiating change. Military personnel, construction workers, and policeman often have this characteristic. They predictably are strong, loyal, take the most direct path from point A to B, and stand for truth and justice. A person possessing this motivator in a weakened state is more prone to violent outbursts

Bruce loved construction work. The contractor he worked for renovated homes. Bruce thrived on demolishing an old home or room and then creating something beautiful in its place. It gave him pride and a sense of accomplishment. He was good at it and had become a foreman in a short period of time. He got paid well, liked the people he worked with, and really enjoyed the physical aspect of his job. The contractor had even talked to him about taking over the business when he retired. So when he got laid off as a result of the weakened economy, it was a shock and a surprise. The recognition and reconstructive opportunities that once fueled him were now unavailable. In an instant, he was disappointed, sad, frustrated, and afraid of the future. He kept looking inward and became narrow-minded and self-absorbed. This ultimately resulted in a violent outburst in an attempt to initiate change.

Following some discussion and an investigation of his assessment results, we began to strategize. It was decided that a long run or bike ride would make a world of difference. This would allow him to release excess negative energy prior to going home.

Our military has had to deal with many challenges. The answers and strategies made available through the use of The Ultimate Life Tool® help to create an easier means of transitioning and traveling through life.

Mirror, Mirror ... *the face of beauty*

What drives men and women to endure pain and expense to feel presentable to the world in which we live? It is obvious, by looking around, that not everyone feels the same way. Is society's standard of what is beautiful dictated by the media?

Yes and no.

As mentioned in the preceding chapter, we are born with factors that motivate us. When fed or fueled, we are happy and energy efficient. When these factors are neglected, we move from their weak aspect, and it's not pretty! One of the goals of self-mastery is staying in the strength of yourself. One of the twelve possible motivating forces available to us has to do with aesthetic beauty. Creating a beautiful environment, presenting well and gaining attention are all ways to feed this force. Many of our movie stars are motivated by this characteristic. They thrive on performing and being in the limelight. Musicians, dancers, artists, interior designers, public speakers, and athletes each have a great need for attention, much like a plant requires more water. When people who possess this motivating factor do not get enough attention, they become self-absorbed and you may begin to hear a lot of "I" statements. Often, the conversation is all about them in an attempt to receive attention. The beautiful thing about this motivating force is that it can be fed by its owner when not available from someone else. This simply means you can feed yourself and you don't have to wait for someone else to guarantee your survival. There are many ways in which we can fuel ourselves. With a stronger requirement for attention, one might find going shopping to be invigorating. Purchasing something beautiful is always a winner. Getting your hair or nails done, getting a massage, having friends over for dinner, dressing up and going dancing, and speaking or performing in front of one or many all work to replenish a much-needed energy supply.

This pilot or co-pilot shows up the most frequently in the human race. We all "come in" with the need for attention; without it, we don't survive. As we age and our drivers become more firmly in place, we begin to see variety in what moves us down the road of life.

The Control Freak

Her days were filled with lists. They were written on Post-it notes, in her calendar, and logically ordered in her brain. She would create a list the night before for the things that needed to be done the following day. It all seemed too orderly and rigid for her family. She planned *everything*. Her husband and two children felt like they were being herded from one place to another with marching orders. There was little room for spontaneity or fun. Sara told me her family called her "Sergeant Mom" as her eyes began to well up. "I hate being called a sergeant! I don't mean to irritate them; it's just that they are so unorganized! I feel as though everything will fall apart if I'm not on top of it. I don't think I am controlling: I am simply creating order in our hectic life."

I asked Sara to give me a rundown of what happens when her kids get home from school. She revealed the following. "Well, I have them empty their backpacks. I look for assignments or papers I am supposed to read. They have a snack and play outside for an hour, weather permitting. Then they come into the house and do their homework. Both Sam and Sondra have soccer two afternoons a week. They are in different age groups, so of course they practice on different fields. If I haven't organized a carpool, I end up darting from field to field, dropping off and picking up. When we get home, I get dinner started and they watch TV or play a video game. After dinner, we all clean up. The kids shower and get ready for bed. If they have a project, we work on that ... if not, they have at least half an hour of reading time before bed." She continued, catching her breath. "I usually have a couple of loads of laundry going while dinner is happening. After the kids are in bed, I fold the laundry and—" I stopped her. This simply sounded like many busy mothers across America, doing it all in an attempt to keep the kids, husband, and household together. In today's busy world, it does take organization to make things happen.

Surprisingly, Sara reported that Sam was thirteen and in seventh grade and Sondra was fourteen and in eighth grade. With the description she gave me, I was under the impression they were in elementary school. This was a great opportunity to go through the Cycle of Life™ with her, revealing the growing needs of the kids. I further stated that continuing to control their every move at this age inhibits personal growth.

I directed Sara's attention to her assessment results. Sara was very meticulous about her surroundings, and one of her drivers required that she stay organized. The likelihood of her becoming manipulative during times of exhaustion was also highly probable. Because of this innate need, those closest to her may often feel as though they're in the military or controlled by unreasonable demands.

I asked Sara how her husband responded to her controlling behavior. She replied, "I told you he calls me a control freak! He openly teases me about it at parties or around our friends. Fortunately, we've been married twelve years, so he is used to it. He knows it is better to throw his hands up and let me have my way." I asked if she noticed him distancing himself over the past few years. She admitted that intimacy was almost extinct, but assumed it was his age and a result of hormonal decline. When I explained that he required something other than organizational skills from his wife, she became concerned. Sara conveyed the desire to make this life more about their relationship rather than just her need to categorize everyone's day from morning to night. Now we could begin.

First, I reassured Sara that she is perfect just the way she is and that with some minor adjustments, their family life would be on track. I reminded her that we tend to look through our own glasses (or our own perspective) when making choices. That is fine if you are single, but she is part of a family, and each person within the family has different things that make them tick. They are energized and motivated by different factors. I explained that when family members take The Ultimate Life Tool® assessment we can see exactly what fuels each person. Their results revealed that her husband was motivated by accomplishment. Sam was motivated by play and optimism, while Sondra was motivated by creating aesthetic beauty. Putting her ability to create order to better use, I suggested she keep these needs in order, thus supporting the growth of each family member. A statement like "Honey, you're right!" goes a long way in reconnecting with her husband. By allowing Sam room to laugh and goof around, he gets to experience play, which fuels creativity and intelligence. Sondra breathes by receiving recognition. Telling her how pretty she looks or praising her work is all it took to re-ignite their relationship as mother and daughter. Everyone felt less judged and more accepted by Sara.

Providing what the family needed was not quite sufficient in meeting Sara's orderly demands. Consequently, I suggested she volunteer for an outside community project or pursue a part-time administrative position that required her natural skill set. Sara let out a sigh of relief. She felt so much better having concrete information to work with.

Chapter Nine

What "ORE" Y.O.U.?

Your Natural Tolerance Levels
Defining the role that personal preferences play in your life and how they are best interpreted by using the analogy of ore.

*O*ur preferences toward ourselves and our tolerance for others are determined by our alchemy. Alchemy is another term used to describe levels of refinement as they relate to the dynamics found in nature. It was a term that referenced an ancient process of turning lead into gold. If this did in fact occur, one would have to alter the molecular infrastructure of the ore itself. Since we can't alter human molecular and cellular make-up, the likelihood of turning a slob into a neatnick is highly improbable. Thus, using the analogy of ore is the most appropriate in that it points to natural elements in terms of languaging a person's tolerance for others and their environment. In addition, it conveys a three-dimensional familiar perception while demonstrating significant value when it comes to personal purpose and career paths. It is this organic understanding of human nature that has stood the test of time. Today, one can see its faint recollection in phrases describing a silk purse and a sow's ear. It seems as if we are never satisfied with what stands before us. The need to improve upon or change something can be greatly influenced by one's alchemy. The higher the alchemy, the more intent the desire to convert or improve upon the object of their attention. This need to turn something into something more in alignment with their personal level of refinement is where we deny mankind his natural purpose. Man possesses an alchemy that has its own inherent potential and its own boundaries of tolerance. We don't want to mess with it, as we will jeopardize the rhythm of life, which produces many gifts. For example, sand to some is quite inconvenient; it gets stuck in your clothes at the beach and seems to leave a trail in the car, the house, and your shoes. However, it offers enjoyment when making sand castles. And when acknowledged for its significance by a true alchemist—a person who can *see* its purpose, we receive the gift of glass. Understanding alchemy cleans the windows of your own perception of life and brings about a realization that everyone is perfect just the way they are. When we see this perfection, a collaborative exchange is achieved and gifts are revealed.

People, places, and things range from a gold to a lead alchemy. High gold may convey obsessive-compulsive behaviors, while a person with a copper alchemy may live in an unkempt environment and consider it bliss. A woman with a gold alchemy will not be well-matched with a mate, a job, a vacation, or a lifestyle that falls into a copper or lead category. When we overlook our alchemy and settle for a situation that puts us outside of our comfort zone, we accept a compromise that we may not be able to live up to. This costs us energy. How long we can remain in another's company is determined by alchemical boundaries. Everyone has their own set of boundaries that differs from those around them, yet frequently we do not understand why one cannot go camping and someone else needs an environment drenched in creature comforts. Understanding one's range of alchemical tolerance dismisses the mystery. This is just one dimension to our human significance. Each category described in the knowledge and quantified by The Ultimate Life Tool® technology identifies the whole of who we are. Even more importantly, once one masters their ability to *see* the nature of another, health, wealth, love, and perfect self-expression become daily companions.

The Three Musketeers ... *sibling rivalry*

One day a woman walked into my office in tears, proclaiming that she was going crazy because her three sons were all so different and her household was in complete disarray. She proceeded to tell me that her eldest son William, who is ten, was a perfectionist. He wanted all of his things neat, clean, and in perfect order. She compared him to Michael J. Fox on *Family Ties,* as he would have worn a suit to school every day if permitted. Her middle son, Charlie, who was eight, was very easy-going and flexible, much like Joey on the sitcom *Friends.* Although he sometimes forgot to brush his teeth before school, most of the time he was pretty well groomed and just went with the flow. Then there was her youngest son, Brandon, age six, who seemed to be the catalyst behind all the chaos in the household. He was very similar to Pigpen on *Peanuts,* and nothing—and I mean *nothing*—was ever picked up, put away, or even thought about again. This drove the eldest son crazy, and in turn, my client was at her wits' end trying to keep the peace.

She went on to explain that Brandon, the youngest, came home from school one day and wanted to get a Game Boy out of his brother William's room. My client and her husband had decided to let William put a lock on his bedroom door so that he could maintain his property just the way he liked. When Brandon was unable to get into the room, he decided to grab a hammer, and began bashing in the door. He then shook the door until he broke off the casing. In his rage, he finally realized that the door had come off its hinges. About this time, the middle son, Charlie, came home and saw what he had done. He threw out a few choice expletives announcing how much trouble he was going to get in when William came home. Charlie then sneaked off to call his dad. When Dad got home, he consoled his eldest son, assuring him he would fix his door, making it as good as new. He made sure that Brandon was punished for his behavior. This is the incident that precipitated Mom showing up at my office.

I proceeded to explain to her that this was all quite normal and that there was simply an alchemical incompatibility between the two boys. I told her that her youngest son has what we call a "copper alchemy". He was more organic and messy by nature. His level of refinement was never going to match William's, but there was a way to cohabitate in peace. I suggested limiting the time they spent together by keeping their activities and personal property separate. They were only able to spend a few hours together and get along. I explained that her middle son Charlie was a really good buffer between the two because he is a "silver alchemy", which made him more flexible, practical, and durable. This made it possible for him to spend extended periods of time with either brother. Charlie was actually the son with the most friends and relationships because he was able to tolerate both "copper" and "gold alchemy" without much effort on his part. William, on the other hand, was very inflexible, fussy, and picky about his surroundings. This made it difficult for him to play in all of the same arenas as Charlie, and he was completely intolerant of Brandon's messiness. Although this would never change, it gave her a different appreciation of her sons, and she was then able to create different ways of respecting each of their preferences.

I went on to explain that William would make a brilliant interior decorator or a Web designer because he had such a wonderful eye for beautiful presentation. Charlie would be a great teacher, because he was able to reach large audiences with ease. Brandon would excel as a camp counselor, farmer, or construction worker. He did very well with hands-on activities and liked to build things. This helped this very frustrated mother truly love and embrace the unique quality of each of her sons. Once she had tapped into what made each boy "tick," she was able to create activities that would help her three sons grow into charming, confident young men.

Sally and the new hire ... *office unrest*

A woman by the name of Sally came to me one day, seeking help in regard to her records-transport business. She had an employee named Martha who had been with her a very long time and was the backbone of the entire operation. Martha was very meticulous, neat, and extremely fussy. She was irreplaceable to Sally, whose business had grown 30 percent in the last year. She needed to hire an errands girl to assist both of them in their day-to-day operations and thought she had found the perfect candidate. Her name was Amy and she had all of the qualifications that Sally was looking for.

The problem began when Sally had Martha and Amy share an office. Martha was to train Amy about daily operations as well as acceptable office appearance and proper protocol. Martha was sixty and Amy was twenty-eight, which I thought was great from an employer standpoint. Martha was reliable and mature, enabling her to handle most situations with ease. Amy was energetic and flexible, which allowed Martha to deal with the intricacies of the business, leaving the physical footwork to Amy.

When Amy was hired, my client hadn't noticed the tattoo on her neck or the purple ends on her jet-black hair. Amy had conveniently pulled her hair back and wore a turtleneck sweater to her interview. When Amy arrived, hair draping over her shoulders and wearing a scoop-neck blouse, Martha had a very hard time holding back her opinions of inappropriateness. In addition, Amy was the earthy type, subscribing to a vegetarian, eco-friendly, and organic lifestyle. Amy chose to skip daily baths to help conserve water and spare the environment of added abuse. It was all Martha could do to hold her tongue. Privately, she would complain to Sally about her misery and never had a good word to say about Amy. Amy was happy as a lark. She went about her daily tasks, leaving piles of work on her desk and rotting food in a receptacle next to her desk to be later added to her compost pile at home. None of this bothered her, and she simply could not understand why Martha was so uptight. The tension between the two officemates mounted, and Sally's business began to suffer. Sally was a big believer in a healthy work environment and could no longer tolerate the tension in the office.

I suggested that the first thing Sally should do is move Amy out of the front office. Allowing each employee to have their own space would relieve the alchemical distension immediately. Martha has what we refer to as a "gold silver alchemy" and this made her less tolerant of Amy's disorganization as well as her lifestyle choices. Amy was what we refer to as a "copper alchemy" which appears as relaxed, organic, and is sometimes viewed as sloppy in it's presentation. This simple solution would benefit both Martha and Amy. Martha could resume her role as the "face" of the company. She could breathe again and regain her sense of a projecting a quality presentation. Creating physical space for each of them would allow them to perform their tasks to the best of their ability while efficiency was restored within Sally's company. This separation would also help them to be more tolerant of one another. I also suggested that Amy's domain should be the back end of the operation. Amy was not afraid to get dirty and enjoyed the physical challenge. Amy would thrive in this environment, and it would minimize her face time with customers, who might take offense to her youthful and colorful presentation.

Alchemical incompatibility is the number-one reason for relationship failure. We often speak about something being out of our boundaries or comfort zone when we are unknowingly referring to "alchemical incompatibility". Once we are aware of these differences, it becomes easier to successfully appreciate and respect one another by using a few simple strategies that the Y.O.U. consulting group has to offer. Today, Martha and Amy work quite well with one another. Although you wouldn't find them socializing, they do respect one another, and the business is benefiting from their healthy partnership and hard work.

Chapter Ten

How do *you* learn and relate?

Defining Your Natural Energy
Describing the order in which you connect with your environment serves to offer answers in being able to identify how to communicate with life on all fronts.

*I*n determining how you connect with the world, it is helpful to identify how you physically transmit electromagnetism. In chapter 11, we discuss how big we are by the width of our wingspan. In the picture of the Vitruvian man designed by Leonardo da Vinci, we are reminded of the many planes that intersect and divide our physicality as we stretch our arms wide open in defining our electromagnetic field. It is this sphere of electromagnetic potential that conducts opportunities to open up to our environment. It brings truth to the phrase, "you are in my space." The way in which we open up and see how a person connects with others is vital in education, sales, and in any situation where immediate communication is desired. One of the wonders of nature is knowing that even your energy field gives off physical clues such as the softness of skin, muscle definition, movement, and stillness as a means of making our physical existence better understood and available to the naked eye.

Being unique means that we connect with our world differently than perhaps our loved ones. Some learn by being in the company of living things, while others cannot download information unless they are moving. Today, many children diagnosed with ADD are asked to sit still while in the classroom. An over-pronounced or hypertrophied moving center is a common denominator when assessing a child or adult with ADD or ADHD symptoms. Asking a moving-centered anything to sit still is simply cruel. Moving centers will *never* learn by sitting still. However, put them on a recumbent bicycle with a book on tape and they will download at the same rate, if not faster, than everyone else in class. It's important to qualify that not all moving-centered children suffer from ADD or ADHD; however, many ADD and ADHD children frequently have over-pronounced moving centers.

Our electromagnetic field is divided into four quadrants, much like the chambers of the heart. Each needs to be activated in a natural sequence, in order for information to be made available for future use. Many people do not retain information because they are not fully integrating the information. Because each human is configured slightly differently from another, knowing the order of how you or others connect can expedite communication. Our energy centers also can change in size depending on the nature of our environmental opportunities or setbacks. Let us take a moving-centered individual, for example. This person talks on the phone while pacing the floor, converses with others while exercising, and listens to music or information on an iPod while strolling the beach at sunset. You will find them tapping their foot at the dinner table, twirling the ring on their finger, or jiggling their leg in church.

They twitch in their sleep and prefer to get up and go rather than sit and contemplate. However, in a situation where the moving center becomes compromised, other centers will strive to balance the physicality of the moment. In the case of a young moving-centered man who sustained multiple injuries in a car accident, his moving center was clinically immobilized with traction devices and various other straps and buckles. His mother would bring books and read to him hour after hour until such time as the moving center began to atrophy and the intellectual center became the doorway to his outside world. We see this in the case of many paraplegics who continue to leave their imprint on this lifetime simply by maximizing the center that is working.

Unfortunately, for many people, it seems that most of life is spent straining to connect with this life we call our world. When we are often faced with an incompatible energy connection, we get discouraged and this makes us feel lonely. Loneliness leads to toxicity. This can happen when an intellectually centered individual tries to connect with a moving center or vice versa. Having to breakdown a few doors to connect with someone or something (a song or speech) can be exhausting and robs us of precious energy that we need to reach our destination or destiny. Very few experiences lend themselves to versatility when it comes to being easily understood. However, with the invention of film, we first began to reach three of four energy centers (excluding the moving center) in one fell swoop. Then with the invention of action films and video rentals, moving-centered people could get up and stretch or move around while the film was in session and participate vicariously through the action-packed movements in the script being played out.

Understanding your energy centers and how you connect is vital to maintaining efficient energy output. Just as it is with the four tires on a car, if one is low or over-inflated, you get poor gas mileage and run the risk of getting into a car accident. The same holds true for *you*. If you are trying to communicate with your teenager and he is moving-centered, go for a walk with him. If he is emotionally centered, give him a hug before talking. There are many things we can do to better communicate. Mastering your ability to see just how to communicate will bring success to the moment. If you are a Realtor and are showing a home to a fairly refined, instinctually centered individual, you'd better show them something that looks good, sounds good, and smells good. It's not a good idea to take them to a home located near a cattle ranch or freeway. The smell of manure or sound of traffic alone will repulse them, and in an instant, they will feel disrespected. "He just didn't get us," is a common complaint when we don't know what we are dealing with.

The following case studies provide classic examples of how energy centers can change the way in which we communicate with each other. Gaining insight into one another breeds unconditional love. Isn't that what we are all looking for anyway? A safe place to be the perfection of who we are without being judged?

My Little Wiggle Fidget ... *when they can't sit still*

Revisiting her daughter's development, Emily began to share how her twenty-year-old daughter Amanda rarely sat still. She shared that her little "wiggle fidget" was a joy and a whirling dervish all in one. She loved to laugh and play every waking hour. When Amanda was small, Emily would read to her before bed. As soon as she finished one book, Amanda would chime in with, "Read me another one!" Emily would read until her mouth went dry, which was usually at the end of the third or fourth story. Emily was aware that at the tender age of three, Amanda was using diversionary tactics so she did not have to go to sleep, but Emily loved sitting with Amanda all cozy in bed. It seemed to be the only time the merry-go-round slowed down. Emily laughed as she described looking back on nights filled with Dr. Seuss and Bernstein Bears. "I still have many of them memorized to this day!" she exclaimed.

When Amanda entered kindergarten, her bright, congenial nature quickly endeared her to her teacher. But it did not take long before Emily was summoned to the class for an after-school conference. This was one of many parent/teacher conferences of this type. Comments like, "You know your daughter is so bright and I do enjoy her, but she is very disruptive," were plentiful. "She cannot sit still. She finishes her assignments right away and then finds the need to help her neighbors. When asked to return to her chair, she sits and rocks in the chair, and I am afraid she will tip over backwards. When all four legs are on the ground, she begins to tap her pencil to a tune no one else can hear. She always scores very high on quizzes, yet never does any work in class or at home. Anytime I leave the room in the care of my teaching assistant, Amanda marches to the front of the class and begins to teach the day's lesson. She is so cute, and more often than not, I find myself hiding my laughter. I think she has ADD, and I was wondering if you would consider putting her on medication to see if it helps her sit still and behave." Emily's heart would sink.

She loved it when Amanda went to kindergarten. This meant a couple of hours a day to herself. Because Amanda was such an extrovert, she required constant attention. It felt as if they were both on the move from morning to night. When they were at home, Amanda was full of questions and demands for attention. At the end of the day, Emily often collapsed into bed exhausted. Sometimes she wished there was a drug that could offer just a few moments of peace. Yet it still saddened her when the teacher suggested medication for ADD. Emily and her husband tried holistic and dietary suggestions, limiting sugars and red dye #40, and serving more protein-rich meals. This resulted in very little change in Amanda's energy or activity levels.

As Amanda progressed through elementary school, Emily became a permanent fixture at the school. She volunteered as a room mother, a reading aide, and treasurer of the PTA, all in an effort to be present, available to assist her teachers and run interference when necessary. When Amanda was in third grade, Amanda's parents decided to try a course of Ritalin. Their once-exuberant and out-of-control daughter could now sit quietly in class. She developed a nice group of friends. Her teacher was most appreciative. Amanda was fine in school, but the teachers did not see the puddle she would turn into after school when the medication had worn off. She was exhausted and irritable. The drug suppressed her appetite, so she didn't eat much during the day. When she got home, her blood sugar was low and so was she. They decided to keep her medicated during the school year and took her off of Ritalin over the summer.

In seventh grade, real trouble began. "Amanda, is your homework finished?" was a common query. "Yes!" was the consistent reply. Even though her mother was at school, her teacher failed to inform her that Amanda was not turning in her homework and that she was close to failing several subjects. When pressed or questioned, the usual reply was, "The teacher is lame. I can teach the class better. Why should I have to do the homework? I get A's on all my tests. I think homework is stupid. School is boring."

These conversations continued throughout the eighth, ninth, and tenth grades, accompanied by numerous strategizing meetings with her teachers and the principal. Amanda no longer found school fun. Her sparkle was gone. By the end of tenth grade, her parents decided to have her take the California High School Proficiency Exam administered twice a year by the State of California. She passed and received her high school diploma at the age of sixteen. She began what is called life skills training. She got a job and a checking account. She paid for her gasoline, and a portion of her paycheck went toward paying us rent. A year later, she enrolled in our local community college and began to thrive. Now at twenty years of age, she is a year away from receiving her four-year degree in communications.

As Amanda settled into her new path in life, Emily embarked upon a new career path: counseling. She was looking for a tool that would help her assess her clients in a more efficient manner. I met Emily at a networking meeting where I was the guest speaker. She responded to my call to action for experts.

Today, we reminisced. She learned The Ultimate Life Tool® takes five aspects of our being into consideration when all other assessments focus on one or two. She realized that Amanda did not have ADD; the way she learned was through movement. Every time she was told to sit still, her brain shut off. She felt horrible that drugs seemed to be the only recourse at the time. There wasn't enough information available at the time. Her new career path now entails helping teachers see the children in their classrooms. Each center is specific to one of the four energy centers. As new concepts are introduced, the class curriculum is asked to accommodate the configuration of each child's method of learning. This methodology is fun and exciting, and drug use can be reduced or eliminated.

Y.O.U. practitioner training and access to The Ultimate Life Tool® technology is not just intended for a select professional group. It is available to all. Whether you are a counselor, teacher, parent, or an individual seeking to improve your relationship with life, The Knowledge of Y.O.U.® and The Ultimate Life Tool® are here to change the heart of mankind from one of judgment to acceptance.

Just Touch Me … *please*

I was enjoying an afternoon visit with my girlfriend Charese. We sat on her patio enjoying the warmth of early summer while we watched the sun close another day. However, this moment of reverence was suddenly interrupted by her daughters engaging in a heated discussion.

"He doesn't want to see me anymore!" cried the younger of the two. "He won't call me back and he says I am too clingy. I'm not too clingy. I just really like being close to him! I thought he liked that and it's a dumb reason to break up with someone." Sobbing followed.

Her sister tried to console her but was little comfort. "I am sorry you are so upset but I've seen the two of you together and you barely give him room to breathe. Maybe he doesn't like being touched as much as you."

"Give me a break!" was the wounded sister's retort. "What guy doesn't like being touched? He probably found someone else." The tears continued to flow.

The sister assured her that she would find someone else. "You are pretty, smart, and athletic, and there are a lot of guys out there who would love the fact that you are a hugger. Me? Not so much."

My girlfriend and I turned to look at one another. We knew her daughter was in pain, but it was difficult to not give a little chuckle despite being privy to her agony. Ahh, yes … young love gone awry. We decided to have a chat on the subject while her daughter sorted through her woe, a process that requires she call every very best friend and cry on their shoulder until such time as she was too exhausted to share anymore.

This kind of rejection scenario is played over and over in life with men and women of all ages. And with each relationship failure, we begin to identify what our needs are—but it can take several relationships to begin to get it right. Wouldn't it be helpful if you knew up front exactly *what* you are? This way, you can make better choices, increasing your chances for success in all relationships.

It was clear that the daughter's broken heart was the result of two conflicting energy centers. Her unique way of learning and communicating with the world around her was through her emotional door or center. Being emotionally centered means she needs to connect with living things like people, plants, and animals. She needs to be physically close to a living being. A warm touch helps her to open up and to feel calm, safe, and accepted. She was correct in saying she needs to be close to her boyfriend. For her, that is true. Now, if her boyfriend's first or second doors where emotionally centered, this need for closeness would not bother him.

The older daughter is more intellectually centered first. Things need to make sense to her. Her demeanor is less demonstrative than her sister's. This may have been the case with the boyfriend. He just didn't get the need for holding hands in the hall. Telling her he cared should be information enough.

This is only one dimension that The Ultimate Life Tool® measures. When comparing relationships of any sort, the hierarchy of energy centers is very telling about how two people communicate. If two people possess energy centers in the exact same order or hierarchy, they stand a greater chance of connecting instantly. Each door flies open with ease. They may feel as though they have known each other forever, even though they just met. Between men and women, this can feel as though they just met their soul mate. You think the same, respond the same, and quite often finish one another's sentences. For some, it even feels like a deja vu.

I suggested to Libby that she have her daughter take the assessment and then schedule a session with me to go over her results. Most young women her age love the process and need the feedback to better understand themselves. It can save a lot of time, energy, and heartache.

Chapter Eleven

Is Your Glass Half-empty or Half-full?

What is your natural polarity?
Recognizing polarity offers tolerance in accepting the bad news first and vice versa, regardless of your expectations and desires.

*T*his chapter addresses what we call polarity. It is the electromagnetic potential that resides within every cell of our body, extending out to the peripheral edges of our own electromagnetic field. Just for a minute, stand up and hold out your arms shoulder height to either side of your body. This wingspan denotes the breadth of your electromagnetic potential. It defines your space. When you sense someone has invaded your space … *this is it!* Leonardo da Vinci created a common figure that is often referenced to as the Vitruvian man.

This popular image in tandem with today's trendy "cracking the code" mentality still serves to illustrate what Leonardo originally intended. And that was to simply let people know, through an artistic rendering, how big or magnetic we are. This definitive force field of sorts serves as a transmitter when processing outside influences. For example, when we speak, the words we choose are filtered through our intuition and then through this band of energy encircling our body like the rings of a solar system or radio waves projecting outward from a telegraph station. These waves produce a frequency and the frequency quality is at the direct effect of our environment, choices, and timing. Maintaining one's integrity is largely dependent on the health of this personal electromagnetic field. This is one place where one's behavior can change from good to bad or one's health can become compromised and placed at risk.

The quality of our life is therefore contingent on the health of our electromagnetic field. If it is weak, one's health and personal performance are affected. Striving to remain effective versus affected is the goal of every human being. However, with all of the false recommendations, cookie-cutter solutions, and quick fixes available, man frequently volunteers for the popular mindset versus the appropriate remedy. There is no popular solution. This is because every man, woman, child, and living thing is its *own* creation. Identical twins even have their own fingerprints and means of uniquely processing life. Each field is different and processes information at a slightly different rate, given their personal physical and mental health, which may or may not be desirable based on the integrity of their electromagnetic field. The difference between a "good seed" and a "bad seed" is often found in examining the clarity of its electromagnetic field.

Our electromagnetic field is that electrical energy that causes our hair to stand up on end when we rub it with a balloon or our socks to crackle when we walk on a nylon carpet. The physicality of who we are generates its own electricity and friction as it interfaces with other things that subscribe to the same physical laws that we do. It is this magnetic quality that allows for us to be seen through the eyes of an X-ray. In addition, this field serves as a runway for perceptivity, and given this, one must come to terms with the words "positive, negative, and neutral." These words have a similar relationship to one's physical presentation of self as protons, electrons, and neutrons have in lighting up a room. The configuration of these personal particles contributes to how a person perceives life. Is their cup consistently half-empty or half-full? Do they see what is working or not working first?

Oftentimes, individuals who are naturally negatively charged (versus magnetically weak) consistently see what is not working first and life as needing some repair. This could be the mother-in-law who you think doesn't like you simply because the first words that come out of her mouth seem critical and judgmental. Negatively charged people get a bad rap as being "killjoys," "party poopers," or "critical." These are the same individuals who rise to critical acclaim for having saved the life of a child in an emergency. They are quick to *see* what is not working so that a solution can be found. This frequently eliminates unnecessary collateral damage or future hardship.

Let us return to the mother-in-law who is negatively charged, meaning she is simply more attuned, programmed, or designed to see what is not working first. She approaches your front door bearing gifts, excited to see her grandchildren. As you open the door, she briefly smiles as she reports, "You need to fix the front gate before the dogs get out." There are no elated greetings or sunny hellos, but instead a seemingly tattling remark. Most sons- or daughters-in-law tend to take this behavior personally as an opinion of inefficiency. The reality is, she has always been this way. When she was young and innocent, it was cute. When she entered young adulthood, it came across as conscientious, but now that she is older, it is regarded as judgmental, contrary, and annoying.

She has not changed; she is the same conscientious (and maybe a little contrary) woman she always was. However, the contrary description is not a polarized quality, but rather it comes from the aches and pains that naturally creep up on us after age fifty.

Negatively charged individuals do extremely well in the medical field as surgeons or in the electronic field as quality-assurance engineers who develop programs to avert viruses. Many of our ecological disasters have been made known by these types of individuals. They bring the necessary to our attention. They save lives, and in many ways, are helping to save the planet.

The unfortunate misunderstanding is that in relationships, their keen sense of needing to fix things can get wearisome with someone who is extremely positively charged. Each of us has a range of tolerance that is unique to us. Knowing what you are and where your boundaries begin and end is very helpful in creating a pleasant life. Harmony manifests from creating tolerant situations for you. If you know you are a *very* positively charged person, attempting to tolerate, sway, or convince someone who is negatively charged to sign up for your way of thinking is insensitive and unreasonable. It will only rob both of you of vital energy, leaving you each with a taste of dislike for the other.

Repulsion results from trying to communicate with someone who is out of bounds or when two actively negatively charged individuals try to impress the other. With this information, referenced as The Knowledge of Y.O.U.®, we educate clients in how to "move" in negotiations and in managing family conflicts. Chances are, not everyone is going to like you, and this even occurs in families. Quite often, there are polarized opposites extending far beyond a point where a "meeting of the minds" can take place. YCG certified practitioners often will refer a client to another practitioner simply because of polarity. This is the sign of a professional. There are many adjustments we can make, but polarity is often the cherry on the sundae, the one thing we can't dismiss in trying to help someone.

Positively charged individuals come across as delightful, and some even seem a bit ditzy or immature at times. "Dumb blonde" jokes serve as the hallmark for the extreme in describing "Little Miss Sunshine." Both men and women fall prey to this over-pronunciation of positive polarization. It is not something that they can change; however, nature will temper it over time. It's a lot like watching an aging hummingbird or butterfly. There is a fragility about their disposition and even a sweetness that may come across as candy-coated if the concentration of positive energy is high.

Most positively charged adults have a fairly tolerable range. They, unlike negatively charged people, always see what is working and may not even notice the broken front gate. Instead, they notice the new flower garden planted on either side of the entrance. Many light up a room with their smile or come bearing gifts like Santa Claus, accompanied by funny stories and joyful belly laughter. They are usually more social than negatively charged people, simply because they are set up for success in this regard. Negatively charged people usually are attracted to positively charged individuals within their range of tolerance. This can add to the "attraction."

Neutrally charged people are easily misjudged as well. Where positively charged people are frequently not taken seriously and negatively charged people are often seen as scrutinizing, neutrally charged individuals may be described as distant, snobbish, aloof, or appear negative simply because they reserve to volunteer their impression or opinion. This hesitancy is often misunderstood.

These individuals see what is working and what is not working simultaneously, and it takes longer to process the outcome. This delay is where they fall prey to being judged. A positively charged person in their company is left feeling like they are not on board, and a negatively charged person is left wondering if they are in agreement.

Polarity is something that fluctuates throughout our lifetime as we try to find ways to regulate the integrity of our electromagnetic performance. The Ultimate Life Tool® technology identifies the nature of one's polarity, and more importantly, their range of tolerance. This becomes extremely helpful in understanding others and your responses to them. We are a complex species when it comes to acknowledging the many parts to us. Understanding all of those parts and the way in which they interface is vital to our being able to know our purpose, stay on purpose, and accomplish our purpose in this short visit called life.

The Businessman and the Cheerleader

Jason was fifty-five years old and Jennifer was thirty-eight. They had been married for twelve years and had three young children. Jason was a highly successful entrepreneur with many businesses to manage throughout the course of a single day. There was little time for the family, and the "separate life syndrome" had already begun to manifest. Jennifer, in an attempt to stay connected, looked forward to his business associates arriving in his library located on the premises of their estate.

She would plan nutritious appetizers and organic drinks to serve while they discussed pending matters. Unfortunately, most were accustomed to bacon-wrapped mushrooms, chicken skewers, and martinis. Jennifer was a breathtaking beauty and looked good in a flour sack, but when she greeted his guests, she frequently wore trendy, hip clothing that exposed her belly and her breasts quite predictably. This embarrassed her husband and pushed him further away.

Jason and Jennifer came to me soon after such an episode. Realizing that Jennifer was in the interval meant my having to educate Jason and Jennifer not only about being in separate phases of life but also about energy management.

As we began to go through a typical session, it became apparent that not only did her bubbly, youthful disposition embarrass him in front of his colleagues, it also brought up issues of jealousy as he watched the others eye her while she fluttered about, serving them. Jason was afraid of getting older and losing her. This only fed his fears. His energy pool was diminishing because of his work demands and insecurities around his marriage.

Meanwhile, Jennifer had enough energy for the whole family— and then some. She was very athletic, artistic, and playful. She had the heart of a crusader and frequently took on activities at her children's school that would better serve the cause of concern. When she did not have enough to do, she poured herself into making a vital contribution to Jason's business world by being the best hostess ever (or so she thought).

When I began to reveal the vast differences in their energy pools, things began to make sense. I charted their statistics so they had a visual of what was going on. She began to realize that the cheerleader in her was far too positively charged for his neutral perspective operating during business hours. She was, in fact, draining him rather than giving him energy. He was distancing from her because the interruptions took energy from him and created insecurities, which robbed him of even more energy.

He began to realize that her energy pool was great for motherhood but not for the office. Jennifer, not wanting to separate from his world, asked what she could do. I made some very obvious suggestions such as be a little more ether-like, serve what they are accustomed to, and dress like an administrative assistant during these times. I told her to enjoy her *fashionista* moments with the kids and girlfriends. She agreed but failed to comply outside of my office. It was not natural for her, and in many ways, this relationship was asking too much of each person.

The Ultimate Life Tool® helps improve relationships by giving individuals a clear picture of themselves, their children, spouse, or business associates. I have been able to help hundreds of people confidently walk in the truth of themselves, yet not all relationships remain intact. If a relationship is ended, each person has a clear picture of his or her true nature and personal gifting. Oftentimes, it is an alchemical incompatibility. Sometimes, it's conflicting motivations or just a misalignment of energy centers, all of which will eventually deplete the energy pool of the marriage.

Why Can't You Get it RIGHT! ... *not measuring up*

Dylan, age thirty, sat before me, dejected. "Why can't I ever get it right?" I was perplexed. Dylan was well groomed, handsome, and successful. He felt he could reach higher heights, but one tape kept playing over and over in his mind. He felt defeated in the midst of his success. "Why can't you ever get it right!" was the ghost that was haunting him. He could do a hundred things right in business and then understandably make one mistake. Instead of focusing on all that he had accomplished, he focused on the one item that haunted him most.

During a session, Dylan shared that is father was a very successful engineer who created failsafe systems for large corporations. He had tons of energy and was a very intense individual. He is what I call a quadruple active or an extreme Type-A personality. His father saw what was not working first and then created solutions. This was perfect for his profession, as he was able to quickly discern a weakness or failure within a system and construct a solution. His father became highly sought after for his keen awareness, and this fed his success and sense of accomplishment. This was great from a business point of view, but it did not translate well within the family structure. It was difficult for his father to shift gears, calm down, and be what Dylan needed: a loving, supportive, positive presence in his life.

Dylan loved his father and wanted to please him, yet that seemed to be an impossible task. Because of Dad's negative perception of all Dylan did, Dylan distanced himself from his father. It is amazing how the parental recordings play loud and clear into our adulthood. I knew I could help Dylan quiet the voice of criticism and validate his unique gifts.

I explained that every individual carries either a positive, negative, or neutral charge. This means you either see what *is* working first, what is *not* working first, or you can see both and weigh them before making a decision.

As technology continues to grow in leaps and bounds, human assessment tools need to experience evolution to meet the growing demands of humanity. If this information had been available to Dylan's father, greater understanding and improved relationships would have been the natural course. Fortunately for Dylan, his generation has this Ultimate Life Tool® to provide improved understanding and harmonious relationships with one's self, in business, and in life.

Adversely, Dylan had a more positive charge and he could not understand why his father was so mean and negative. I showed Dylan that his father saw what was *not* working first in every situation at work and at home. Of course, his father thought this was a huge asset and that he was helping make his son a better man. Not once had it entered his mind that his particular approach to life was detrimental to his child. As I looked at Dylan, his entire countenance changed. His eyes welled up with tears as he finally realized that his father's expression of life was simply different and misunderstood. He was able to see the true nature of his father. It is wonderful when nature casts so much light on a long-held pattern of belief.

Dylan left my office feeling ten pounds lighter. He could embrace his successes and shrug off his minor failures. His heart was free of the bitterness and anger he had held toward his father for so many years.

I continue to both appreciate and be amazed by the depth and breadth of The Ultimate Life Tool® and how it can truly improve relationships in all areas of life.

Chapter Twelve

Y.O.U. Morning, Noon, and Night

Recognizing when you are not yourself
Making appropriate choices based on your unique presentation of self.

*N*ow that the many parts that influence our performance begin to make sense, one can see just how unique and special we are. One may look and behave similarly to another, yet the way in which they connect with their world and the level of refinement that they require in order to stay long term may differ dramatically. These less-obvious subtleties are often masked, overlooked, or dismissed. Unfortunately, they hold the key to longevity. If one is hiring someone for a long-term position, inappropriate placement will result in quick turnover. Likewise, in a courtship, subtleties are often clothed in "best learned" versus natural behavior. This results in comments like, "They weren't that way in the beginning," or perhaps, "I didn't get that from their résumé."

In review, we know that learned behavior is not natural behavior. It takes energy from you; performing naturally *gives* you energy. Natural performance is a reflection of *all* of *you*. It's not just about your active or passive nature, your need for flexibility, your talent for creating order, your natural capability to lead, your sensitivity to sound, your perceptivity in identifying what is not working, and your fragility. It's about managing what energy you have in this moment and each moment that follows. It's about getting *you* wired so that self-management becomes nature manifesting at its best. Understanding the *nature* of *you* allows you to maximize your energy output. By being respectful of yourself in managing yourself, you become an asset to yourself, society, and mankind.

When you participate in The Ultimate Life Tool® assessment process, you learn more about yourself than anyone or anything could ever provide. It is an assessment of your true nature. This means that it objectively provides a multi-dimensional understanding of how you operate, what you require to be healthy, and how healthy you are. Unlike most assessments, you will not be decidedly inappropriate for a role or job or relationship; instead, you will be given recommendations that will allow you to maximize your energy within the demands of that desire or situation. YCG practitioners are taught to set their clients up for success.

So let's take look at *self-management* as it relates to time. Remember, we have a shelf life, and the quality of our life is largely determined by how we manage what we came in with.

The Executive Decision ... *understanding your employees*

Quite often you will find companies and/or organizations that are thriving, yet the executive team may experience internal challenges that become disruptive to the daily flow of their organization. The information that The Ultimate Life Tool® reveals can bring clarity and understanding to personnel issues, as well as create positive action. Let's see how an executive assessment can move an organization down the road with fewer bumps along the way.

The Y.O.U. Consulting Group, home of The Ultimate Life Tool® technology, was contacted by Max Art, Inc., a thriving company that makes porcelain figurines and ships them around the world. They needed assistance in three specific areas. Their executive team consisted of six men and one woman. The woman (Cecilia) was the director of human resources. The men were considering releasing her, as she was unable to respond to their needs in a timely manner, as she did not move quickly enough for them. Upon comparing their individual assessment results, the reason for their frustration became obvious. If you recall, each of us has energy centers, yet they present in varying order and intensity. Energy centers are how we learn and connect with the world around us. All six males on the executive team were primarily moving-centered. This means they were on the go and had little patience. They would run into Cecilia's office, bombard her with questions, and then expect an immediate answer. Cecelia's results revealed that she was primarily emotionally centered. This means she loves to connect with living things such as people, plants, and animals. She was keenly aware of her surroundings and created a comfortable environment for both herself and the employees who came to see her. Her emotional center and their moving were not communicating. In short, they did not speak the same language.

When we revealed her natural talent for connecting with others, Cecelia was clearly identified as the perfect person for the HR position. She was both compassionate and sympathetic. She was able to sit quietly, listen, and create a safe place for those who entered her office. She was passive and positive in nature. She was very intelligent, yet processed information in a very deliberate manner. Cecelia saw what was working first. The information confirmed to the men that Cecelia was the perfect fit as the HR director. Cecelia became aware that she needed be ready to move when her male counterparts arrived in her office with a mission to complete.

The second issue that needed to be resolved was the fact that many of their international accounts were unhappy with Jim, the top U.S. salesman. They complained that he was pretentious and they had a difficult time connecting with him. This, in turn, was frustrating for the salesman, as he was not meeting with the success he was accustomed to. Upon examining Jim's Ultimate Life Tool® assessment results, the most obvious factor was his extremely high alchemy. Like people, countries, cities, hotels, cars, and animals also possess an alchemical range of tolerance. The United States is a "silver/gold" country. This worked perfectly for Jim. He was greeted with open arms when he arrived in his designer suit, starched shirt, and silk tie. In the United States, Jim came across as a successful, knowledgeable, and trustworthy soul. Clients knew he would produce what he had promised and the products would be exquisitely crafted. However, his ability to connect with countries having a lower level of refinement became compromised. They found him pretentious, seemingly self-centered, and overdressed for the occasion. It was recommended that the company hire a new salesperson with a more acceptable level of refinement, specifically a "silver" level of refinement. They would be able to connect with their clients with ease and forge a friendly, trusting relationship. This solution allowed Jim to thrive in the domestic market while the new salesman tackled the international marketplace.

The final bump in the road that needed smoothing existed between the studios where the figurines were painstakingly made and the warehouse where they were packaged and shipped. The employees/artists who made the figurines had a "gold alchemy", and each piece they produced was a work of art. They took pride in their ability to get the job done correctly the first time. Their prized creations were taken to shipping— where the violation of property began.

"Copper" is an appropriate alchemy for a shipping department. This group does not require a meticulous setting. Nor do they value the love and care that created the product. The items frequently arrived broken as a result of poor packaging and handling. The shippers would bring them back to the studio with an, "Umm, sorry this got broken. I guess you'll have to make it again." As you can imagine, this would send the creators of fine art into a tailspin!

It was recommended that an intermediary step be added before the final product arrived in shipping. The figurines would be picked up from the studio and taken to a packaging area with employees who possessed a higher level of refinement. They would carefully package each item and hand carry them to shipping. This step resulted in a 30 percent decrease in breakage prior to leaving the studio. This translates into positive cash flow.

The executive team at Max Art, Inc. was thrilled with the solutions the Y.O.U. Consulting Group was able to provide. They had a better understanding of what made each one of them tick and how to interact in a kind and productive manner. The employees were happy, absenteeism decreased, and productivity increased. Their international presence grew and increased in strength and profitability. The decrease in breakage significantly improved their bottom line. All of this manifested without making it anyone's fault.

THE KEY ... *raising a special needs child*

Oftentimes, we are blessed with a life challenge that pushes our growth envelope. Sometimes it surfaces as a career setback, the loss of a loved one, or the challenge of raising a physically or mentally challenged child. Regardless of the strained circumstance, everyone is at the effect of it for with this extraordinary presentation of human nature comes extraordinary life requirements. These initial seemingly subtle demands involve anyone and everyone who is charged with meeting the needs of the child. And to add urgency to the mix, the knowledge that this child only has so much time before he or she needs to become somewhat self-sufficient as a thriving adult leaves parents and siblings stressed and anxious on a daily basis. To date, I have only assisted four families with special needs children. Because of the demands placed upon all family members, advisors specializing in this area of treatment can rarely take on more than a few clients and still have enough time to devote to others attempting to manage life in general.

It was fall of 2007 when I first received a call from Madison Heinz. She had heard about our technology and my unique perspective on life. She was curious as to whether or not this technology—that afforded one the ability to see the authentic nature of another—would have anything in the way of "solutions" to offer her in trying to create opportunities for her child— something that could actually enhance his growth potential.

Gavin, her eight-year-old son, was becoming very hard to handle, and teachers were beginning to complain. They had tried homebound and special education, all of which seemed to run their course in terms of patience and tolerance. I explained to Madison that her son was no different than any other child experiencing repulsive situations. Because of his unique presentation of self, the likelihood for him to encounter repulsion or manifest it was far greater. Children who suffer from what I like to call "modern anomalies" (meaning an unusual or less normal presentation of self, resulting as a toxic imposition of the nature of this century) frequently perceive what is not working first and are far more active or noticeably more passive and withdrawn than other children. Everything that we see in a typical child is exaggerated in their presentation. Understanding what you are looking at, in terms of meeting the demands of the anomaly, becomes critical in achieving success. In revisiting the metaphor of the lion and the rabbit, it is important to recognize that an autistic or ADD rabbit would be extremely withdrawn and non-participative, where an autistic or ADD lion would be quite the contrary; it would be extremely disruptive in most situations. Either manifestation is received as a negative influence with regard to social acceptance. This is largely due to the way that they electromagnetically interface with the range of normalcy pre-established by this lifetime. Understanding where each special needs child intersects with this lifetime can change their course of growth and development dramatically. A developmentally challenged child living on a farm in Tennessee during the early 1800's had far more that he could relate to and benefit from than today's children. Life was much slower, and the chaos that we, as a species, bring to this lifetime is far more distracting and confusing to those who see life from a much purer, natural, primitive perspective. This is the case for the special needs child. They are purer in a sense, as their ability to disseminate a chaotic lifetime is simply not possible. Instead, they rely on the obvious and the true nature of all that exists in an effort to make sense of a blinded society. In many ways, they have greater access to common sense than their counterparts. As parents, we owe it to the child to create non-toxic situations that are free of chaos and filled with self-appropriate opportunities to connect with nature.

I explained to Madison that because Gavin was more active in nature and possessed a well-pronounced organic preference for life, he would develop much more fully if given the opportunity to move and interface with animals. This realization came after several lengthy observatory onsite visits with the family and his teachers. Prior to meeting Madison and Gavin, I had been introduced to the Elfin Forest Saddle Club for special needs children in Southern California. This was the perfect outlet that Madison and Gavin needed. After six months of horseback riding lessons with other kids challenged by similar anomalies, his progress both physically and socially was unbelievable. Like the lion, he needed a place to run. In many ways, he was a stallion seeking a place to belong. This newfound freedom of self-expression not only helped him develop a new skill set that is transferable to other areas of life requiring personal self-management, it also created a family outlet where all family members could participate or find some quiet time in which to reconnect.

Knowing what we are looking at is the key in designing a life path for a special needs child. Not all children, special needs or otherwise, respond to horseback riding. Consequently, knowing what is appropriate saves time, money, and anxiety. The Ultimate Life Tool® affords experts the ability to target specific solutions rather than always trying new modalities to see if they will work. It gives them an initial frame of reference to work from, rather than throwing popular clinically proven recommended "spaghetti against the wall" in an attempt to see what sticks. In the case of working with special needs children, one must consult a YCG Level V certified practitioner to conduct this type of assessment, as it requires an integrated understanding of the knowledge as well as mastering the ability to see human nature without technological input. Not all special needs children can take an online test. This means the ULT® consultant must be able to see with his or her own eyes the nature of the child under observation.

Chapter Thirteen

Intelligence Reports

Leading pioneers in the understanding and application of the Knowledge of Y.O.U.® and The Ultimate Life Tool® technology chronicle pathways to success.

*E*very generation produces great leaders and great teachers. The following pages provide a glimpse of such individuals who are committed to creating a better world of understanding for the generations to come. Each has taken the time to contribute his or her perspective and well-integrated understanding of the technology and the knowledge that supports its performance. They are trained professionals, and many are highly skilled in the application of The Ultimate Life Tool® instrument; others have experienced great change for the better using the tool as a means of gaining clarity, both personally and professionally. Consequently, all of these individuals hold a vision of global promise for the instrument's growth.

The Ultimate Life Tool® is often referred to as "The Green Human Assessment Technology." With everyone going green, the trend is to qualify to participate as an advocate in this regard. Green being somewhat synonymous with intelligence versus ignorance, simply refers to getting back to a better understanding of our true nature. Realizing that *nature* does not make mistakes (while man does), by using The Ultimate Life Tool®, we can identify *what* we truly are, not just what our résumé, upbringing, or lineage implies.

The common theme that rings true throughout this chapter (purposely entitled Intelligence Reports) is one of gaining a new understanding of common sense.

Common sense is the purest form of intelligence; it requires only an understanding of physicality and the laws that govern it. It is not born of words or technological theory, but rather of sight. Currently, as we all strive to regain our ability to see the truth of our own physical significance, we frequently buy into subjective opinion. Today, after wading through centuries of toxic encounters, we have essentially become the blind leading the blind. The following commentaries will provide an opportunity to see how the applied understanding elicits intelligence in conducting daily life and managing the challenges that are a predictable part of being human.

An Objective Perspective

Lisa Nelson
Vice President of Program Development
YCG Master Practitioner and Trainer

As a professional educator, consultant, and coach, I have been in the business of helping others improve the quality of their lives for twenty years. Until four years ago, I had spent a significant portion of my own life seeking out ways to better understand myself. I did this because I truly believed then (and still believe today) that I have a responsibility to present myself from a place of clarity in order to most effectively connect with my clients and students. Consequently, I spent many years immersing myself in the quest of self-discovery. If you checked out my bookshelves, you would see that they are lined with self-help books. I've spent hundreds of hours over the years attending seminars and I've jumped on the bandwagon of many of the various "self-improvement" movements. I would get excited and "motivated" with each new bit of information that rang true for me. But as time passed, the excitement would fade and I would find myself back to square one. I would ask myself, "What was this understanding for which I was searching?" When I couldn't answer that question, I stepped right back on the merry-go-round and started all over again. Four years ago, I stepped off that merry-go-round. I finally found the understanding about myself that was missing through The Ultimate Life Tool® technology. I realized that I had spent those previous years not seeing what was right in front of me the entire time. Even though some of the information I had gathered over the years was useful for me, overall it never quite filled the bill. Most of it came from another's subjective perspective of what they thought would work for me, and because of this, much of it didn't work for me at all. I simply became shrouded in a whole lot of information. The Ultimate Life Tool® technology draws from a body of knowledge called *The Knowledge of Y.O.U.® or Your Own Understanding.* This knowledge addresses what lies in the obvious as it relates to each one of us and our physicality. It shows us why we do things the way we do and how each one of us is wired slightly differently when it comes to reasoning. It shows us how we spend our time and energy and where we should spend it based on our style and level of refinement. It also shows us the importance of responding to magnetic influences in our lives. Understanding myself through The Ultimate Life Tool® technology allowed me to take the veil away and see myself for the very first time for the unique individual I am ... and it allowed me to honor myself in every way.

Today, I am completely able to understand, accept, and love myself. I no longer try to attempt to change myself or try to fit into something that just will not work for me. Because of The Knowledge of Y.O.U.® and The Ultimate Life Tool® technology, I now know exactly what works for me. I know what drives me and how to fuel that drive; I know how to surround myself with people and opportunities and activities that keep *me* moving forward effectively, and I do this every day. Furthermore, I know how to make successful, authentic connections with others, and this has given me the ability to enhance all of my relationships. But most of all, I know myself. The peace of mind this has given me has freed my energy to focus on what I am rather than what I am not. The Ultimate Life Tool® technology truly does transform lives. I know this because it has transformed my own life and I am dedicated to sharing this possibility with others.

As a master practitioner and trainer in The Knowledge of Y.O.U.® and The Ultimate Life Tool® technology, I am able to come from a place of understanding about my clients and students the instant they walk into my office because I can *see* them. Remember, this capacity to *see* is coming from an objective perspective. This unique body of knowledge gives me a tool to assist them in realizing how it is that they show up in this world, naturally, and what that means in terms of their unique potential. It gives me the ability to effectively connect with their individual needs. I don't have to try to help my clients and students figure out why something isn't working in their lives. Based on how it is that they show up through this technology, when something isn't working, I can see why it isn't; together, we can identify specific things that they can do to turn it around. Like I was, many of my clients and students are simply searching for ways to better understand themselves. Just like the operating manual that comes in the glove compartment of your car, The Ultimate Life Tool® technology presents you with your very own operating manual that is unique to you and will assist you in moving forward at your optimum.

The beautiful aspect of this technology is that it not only helps people to understand themselves and how they operate, it gives them the ability to honor themselves. So many people waste their precious energy beating themselves up because they are not where they think they should be in life or they are unhappy in their relationships or they can't seem to take that next step. Coming from a place of understanding through The Ultimate Life Tool® technology, life itself starts to make sense. Awareness begins to replace the judgment people place on themselves and others. This gives them the ability to fully realize how to make better connections in their relationships and even when they perhaps need to disembark from a relationship. And it gives them the ability to see those next steps they need to take to continue to move forward and actually take them.

Most of us have experienced frustration with others not understanding why they do things the way they do and some experience these same frustrations with themselves. Understanding Y.O.U. assists you in making your relationship with yourself and others more conscious and appropriate. The Ultimate Life Tool® technology reveals the unique perfection that is you and gives you the ability to honor yourself and others the way Mother Nature intended ... naturally.

Men on a Mission

Hal Taylor
Safety Engineer YCG Board President
YCG Certified Practitioner

Men, we need this knowledge. Women get this innately and men often don't get it at all. Women love this knowledge—*and* we need men to understand this knowledge, embrace it, and use it so that we can bring peace to the world in which we live.

I have always been fascinated by why people do what they do, how people get to where they are in life, and how they discover their potential and live life to the fullest. Then there are people who wallow in horrid mediocrity, who never achieve great heights.

It's an amazing feeling to be cruising through life. When you are hitting on all cylinders, you are in the flow; life seems effortless, and everything is working for you. When you have that rush of knowing that you are doing what you were put on this earth to do, and you are doing it at a high level, time stands still. You look at the woman in your life and feel love like you've never before. You look in the eyes of a child and know why you were put here. You are lost in the moment.

Athletes call it "the zone." This is where the basket is *huge* and you can see the seams on the curveball as it comes toward you. You know you are going to make the basket and hit the ball out of the park. It seems like the other players on the field are all moving in slow motion, and you are running the court at full speed. You can see the field and know what your opponent is going to do before they do it. A musician closes his eyes and gives himself over to the moment while tens of thousands of people in the audience scream in adulation; it's as if his song is playing itself.

How do you get those moments? We've all had them at one time or another. How do you get more of them? How do you get them all of the time? How do you get to a place where you consistently understand yourself and the people around you, and are able to anticipate their next sentence or movement? This is where the friction of relationships is diffused, leaving things to operate more smoothly and efficiently at a high level.

Why does someone who seemingly has it all sabotage it? Why is it people make poor decisions that undo the great things in their life, their business, marriage, or relationship with their child? And then, the best story of all is how someone overcomes insurmountable odds, gains wisdom and insight, and redeems themselves to soar to even greater heights.

Knowing Y.O.U. is the difference between dancing through life with ease to your own music versus slugging it out every step of every minute that you are here. You may get to the same place in the end, but one is blissful and wonderful and energizing; the other eventually just wears you out.

I've been in the personal development field for about twenty years, and human behavior is my passion. I've managed people for years, on small and large teams all over the world, and I've gotten the best out of people using one simple principle: find out what drives them and fulfills them and they will unlock their talent. They will give their all to the team and always come back wanting to do more. How do you find out what drives them and fulfills them? This book and this knowledge unlocks that mystery. It will help you understand why people do what they do, and how to get the best out of people. It's not about *changing* anyone; it's about unlocking that amazing potential that is in everyone *and* bringing it from potential to reality, thus utilizing that talent for the greater good.

I am an engineer by education. I am all about getting the maximum efficiency out of a system or an organization without overstressing or overtaxing it. I've hired people based on this knowledge. It has been accurate every time. It helps me to make the slightest adjustment in dealing with someone, creating a result that turns them into a high-performing superstar.

I have used this with my family and loved ones. It has helped me heal family relationships simply by understanding the dynamic and the specific attributes of them. It has made me infinitely more accepting and less judgmental. Believe me, I used to specialize in judging people and always seemed to be frustrated when people wouldn't change into what I wanted them to be. Now I understand why they do what they do. In respecting this, I help them unlock what's inside so they can better understand their purpose.

This tool helps you understand Y.O.U. It will help you know why you flow in some areas of your life and struggle in others. You can use The Ultimate Life Tool® to structure your life so that it flows smoothly and effortlessly most of the time. The knowledge in this book makes the world a better place.

Again, women get this knowledge, while we boys are a little behind the curve. Many men perceive growth as going from an eighteen-foot boat to a twenty-four-foot boat. Guys, there's more to it than that. You need to understand this knowledge and how to use it to create more in your life. That includes fulfilling your woman wildly while unlocking your potential and hers. In business, you will be able to work more fluidly and effortlessly. It is time we stop guessing and start *knowing* the relationships we are in. Imagine having the ride of your life *and* the fulfillment of creating the perfect relationship with your woman, your children, your family, and your business

<u>Saving Grace</u>

Dr. Beth Wade

Vice President of Community Outreach

YCG Master Practitioner and Trainer

The Knowledge of Y.O.U.® and The Ultimate Life Tool® gave me new life and saved my healing practice. I am honored that I can share my story with you and hope you can relate to and be inspired by the importance of this revolutionary technology.

I began my second career at forty-nine years of age after the loss of my husband. I returned to school to earn my master's in divinity and PhD in metaphysical sciences with the intention of beginning my practice at the completion of this goal. Because I love to be challenged and check things off "the list," this is exactly what I did. Of course, starting a new business is a large undertaking that I expected to flow with ease. Fortunately, along with my high expectations, I am persistent as well. I took a deep breath and chose to enjoy the journey. Eventually, all did fall into place with a beautiful office, promotional literature, Web site, and advertising. My clientele grew and we experienced great healings and personal growth. Yet I felt an underlying dissatisfaction. I knew I had a gift with the ability to identify the client's imbalance and had succinct methods or suggestions to get them moving freely upon their path in life. So why weren't they taking the simple steps to make their life easier? I also had occasion to interact with certain clients without establishing healthy boundaries. This resulted in unmet expectations and miscommunications. After a year and a half of this activity, I was discouraged, disillusioned, disgusted, and ready to throw in the towel.

"How can this be?" I would lament. I worked so hard to establish a proactive health practice. The ideas are great, the methods are sound—and I am most unhappy. I knew I was called to assist the human condition and that I was made for this sort of work; I began to look around and asked God for help.

Part of starting a new business and creating a consistent message is the importance of being face forward in the community. I attended several networking groups and was present at important events about town. At one of these gatherings, I had the good fortune of meeting Dr. Zannah Hackett, founder and leading authority on The Ultimate Life Tool®. We hit it off instantly and developed an easy rapport. She began sharing her life's work with me and that with this knowledge I would be able to "see" the person standing in front of me. I could actually be freed of criticism and truly understand what moves a person forward in life. Are they active or passive? How much energy do they possess to accomplish the tasks in life? What fuels their body? What is their sense of refinement and how important is this in creating success in relationships? My heart started beating faster and I knew I needed this understanding both for myself and others. As you are aware, the student becomes the master. So I bit the bullet and registered for Level I, II, and III practitioner training with the hope and prayer this would be the key to my own self-mastery and I'd enjoy my practice once again.

Today, I am free, alive, validated, and seen! Because of the depth and breadth of this technology, that is founded in nature and grounded in science, I walk in the joy and freedom of simply being me! Yes, I do process information rapidly, I am highly perceptive, I do see what isn't working first (and that is an asset), I do possess a panoramic view and want a balance that is beneficial to all. I have a level of refinement that allows me to move in a variety of settings with ease, and I have many friends. I am aware of how much energy I have to work with, so I am able to make good decisions about the commitments I am willing to make. I know the quickest way to my heart and how to connect quickly with those around me. Most importantly, I know what feeds my soul. I no longer have guilt and I am able to express my needs to family and friends with kindness and clarity. For the first time in my life, I truly love the vehicle that is me. I possess self-esteem, self-confidence, and I am at peace.

Before a client walks through the door, I know what makes them tick. I have the opportunity to give them their personal operating manual. I get to share their magnificence and that they have a unique purpose on this planet. I have the opportunity to "see" based on objective, scientific information their areas of strength and weakness. Because of this body of knowledge I get to "see" my clients through their glasses or perspective. I get to love and understand the unique being that is before me. I have the ability to communicate this information to them in a way that they are able to receive, download, and assimilate.

I founded The Genesis Center in Carlsbad, California to help individuals and families successfully navigate the many challenges in life. I use The Ultimate Life Tool® to identifying natural traits and characteristics influencing personal performance. Reconnective healing creates balance in the person as a whole, achieving mental, physical, emotional, and spiritual well-being. Combining these two groundbreaking technologies will change the quality and outcome of your life.

<u>Connecting Education with the Ultimate Tool for Life</u>

Edward Abeyta, PhD
Staff Advisor, Board of Regents, UC;
Registrar and Director, Academic Services
University of California, San Diego Extension

The Knowledge of Y.O.U.® and The Ultimate Life Tool® is a life enabler. After working in adult education for over twenty years, I have found that the foundation for any educational endeavor begins with a clear sense of self. As some may say, "How can you help others if you are unable to help yourself?" The Ultimate Life Tool® provides a unique and multi-dimensional framework to enable anyone to view themselves and the others in the world differently. After studying and utilizing various traditional and non-traditional assessments, I have found that most are limited in the broad dimensions of human engagement and significance. As such, no assessment has been able to find the interlocutory connection between oneself, others, and educational pursuits. After utilizing The Knowledge of Y.O.U.®, I have also found that gaining my own personal operating manual has not only reinforced who I am but how I view others in my world. It is with this knowledge that I have been able to gain a clear perspective of who I am and how I see others. It has also provided me with the tools to understand the rationale behind how this translates to my goals in adult education.

As a professional in the field of adult education, I have found that more and more adults are coming to terms with the reality of the global economy that has been foreshadowed for years but is now a reality. In response, adults are ill-equipped to respond. This is not because they lack the aptitude or skill sets; it is because they have been unable to gain the foundation principle of themselves that the Knowledge of Y.O.U. provides. In the adult education field, the answer to the question of why adults participate in learning activities will probably never be answered by any simple formula. Motives differ for different groups of learners at different stages of life; most individuals have not one but multiple reasons for learning. Whether there is a general tendency for people to have a characteristic stance toward learning that is, a learning orientation compelling them to seek learning opportunities to grow personally and vocationally is a question that is partially answered by the enabling power that the Knowledge of Y.O.U.® provides. This knowledge provides the foundation for a person, at any life stage, to not only see others in a different manner, but how to gain knowledge that can be applied in a more meaningful way. This includes responding to a growing global competitive economy.

With the growing need in a globally competitive economy to increase, sustain, and develop employee skills, the role of continuing education in America is more important than ever. Corporate human resource professionals assume increased responsibility to integrate use of training and development, organization development, and career development to improve individual, group, and organizational effectiveness. To carry out their professional duties, most adult working professionals are aware of the importance of maintaining, broadening, and raising their competencies through ongoing education to match the accelerating pace of global economic, social, and technological changes. What is often missing is an educational facet tied to oneself. It is with this knowledge that one can be most effective in personal and professional life and professional pursuits.

The Knowledge of Y.O.U.® is an enabler providing an effective and responsive understanding of the characteristics, needs, and aspirations before investing in any educational endeavors. Each of us must know what we are working on and why this knowledge is so powerful—because it answers the question of *why.* Many adults enroll in educational programs with already-established lives, bringing with them far more experience and practical information than younger students. They are interested in knowing how new knowledge relates to what they already know so they can create a framework within which they can make sense of the new information. Moving from a dependent student role toward a role as an independent and engaged learner is the adult student's first step to taking responsibility for his or her education and answering the question of *why,* regardless what stage one may be in their life.

Providing education to adults at various life stages in adulthood is increasingly important because of globalization, shifting job markets, and transformations in the family, among other things. It is crucial to learn how these changes affect adults' preparedness for the social and economic complexities of an ever-changing diverse world. Given the various obstacles and demands adults face in adulthood, it is important to emphasize that The Knowledge of Y.O.U.® is a personal operating manual that can assist addressing challenges and opportunities that occur at various points in life.

Many people seek to relinquish old dreams and generate new ones throughout their lifetimes. This is a natural development process that provides the opportunity for people to create new situations in the present, new hopes for the future, and new ways to realize those hopes. To accomplish this process, people go through transitions that encompass a point where a change is made: a period of transition followed by development of a new beginning. This process is repetitive throughout the lifespan. Adults face not only transitions in their workplace, but also have to address other transitions in their lives that include but are not limited to managing a family, spouse, aging parents, and more.

Formal education is just the beginning of one's learning. An adult today is far more able than the youth to know, to understand, to explore, to appreciate, to discern subtle relationships, to judge, and to look behind the surface of things to their deeper meaning. The ability of adults to place learning opportunities and life experiences within the context of previous education (both formal and informal) tends to emerge, but the question remains: How do these life experiences tie to any meaning and understanding of oneself? It is through enabling the Knowledge of Y.O.U. and The Ultimate Life Tool assessment technology that completes the full picture of oneself. As such, the foundation for any educational pursuit, in my opinion, must first start with fully understanding the internal dimensions of self and how they connect with everything else in life.

The Businesswoman in a Man's World

Christine Hughes
Vice President of Planning and Promotion
YCG Certified Practitioner

I am a strong woman. I am smart, confident, energetic, direct, and organized. I own both a construction company and a designer glass company. Although I was experiencing success to the outside world, my personal world was spinning out of control. I would get up at 4:30 AM every day to take a walk, knowing I would not see the light of day for the next fourteen hours. As a female in a male-dominated field, I felt as though I had to fight for respect. I would make good decisions and be met with lackluster looks and a slow response to my requests. Because of this, there were frequent angry outbursts in an attempt to establish my expertise and authority. I would arrive at home exhausted with yet another "list of things to do" to keep my family fed, happy, and moving forward. I would thrive on the energy of stress, and when it became too much (which was just about daily), I turned to alternate means of quieting my busy mind. As days, months, and years of this level of activity transpired, I was desperate for a fix. My business was thriving, but my family and I were disconnected. We were not enjoying the fruits of my labor. This is when I attended a networking event where Mr. David Hackett presented information on The Knowledge of Y.O.U.® and The Ultimate Life Tool®. His presentation was intriguing and I knew I had to learn more.

Upon speaking with him after the meeting, he recommended I see his wife, Dr. Zannah Hackett. She is the leading authority on The Knowledge of Y.O.U.® and I was excited about being able to go directly to the source.

What I learned about myself after taking The Ultimate Life Tool® was the beginning of a transformation for myself, my family, and my business. I am able to honor the person I am. My physical being naturally commands authority. I learned I have a high sense of refinement, and that is why I demand excellence from my employees. I learned I process information in a variety of ways, and I have a large energy pool. I also learned how to use my energy wisely. I was honored when Dr. Zannah saw such potential in me that she signed me up to become a practitioner. She knew that a more in-depth understanding of this knowledge would make a big difference in my life—and that it has!

With this knowledge, I was able to restructure my organization so it would run more smoothly. I needed a person of authority under me who the employees would answer to. This person is a well-respected man in the construction field. He is firm yet fair, and the employees respond favorably to him. I hired an office manager, which took more off my plate and allowed me to work fewer hours. I rearranged some of my employees to positions that better suited their areas of expertise. They were thrilled with the change and have become happier and more productive because I was able to "see" their attributes and reward them.

As I trusted these decisions, I was able to relax and let go of micromanaging. I'm more relaxed at home and can be present for my loved ones. I can work out when I choose, not only at 4:30 AM. I am kind and patient because I know what motivates the people in my immediate sphere of influence. I have never been happier.

I am honored that as a Level III Practitioner, I am able to present various aspects of this knowledge, just as David Hackett had done. I am dedicated to bringing The Knowledge of Y.O.U.® and The Ultimate Life Tool® to the world. Not long ago, I was angry and overworked. Now my world is in order, I am balanced, and I am called upon to share the beauty of this knowledge with prospective clients and new practitioners. I am honored to be a part of the YCG team as we make a permanent place for this advanced human technology in business, home, and life.

The Gift
Saundra Pelletier
YCG Certified Practitioner
Author and Speaker

We are all informed by our early experiences with family and friends. My youth was spent in a small town, where even as a small child, I felt impatient in some way that I couldn't articulate, even to myself. It was just a feeling that dwelled deep and true within my psyche. I think my mother sensed this restlessness, and she was determined that I would explore the world beyond Caribou, Maine. Part of her strategy to ensure that I would experience more from life was to prohibit me from participating in any kind of domestic activity. I was not permitted to set the table or sweep the floor, wash a dish, or even make my bed. And home economics class was definitely not on my school agenda. She even had me carrying a mini-sized briefcase to kindergarten, hoping that this would plant the seed to want to explore larger opportunities.

My mother instilled in me confidence and self-acceptance and a belief that there was nothing I couldn't achieve. What a gift! So it wasn't surprising that I was ready and eager for adventure. I embraced college with enthusiasm. I naturally thrived in this atmosphere and took part in many extracurricular activities, where I discovered a natural proclivity for interacting with groups of people with ease. There wasn't a shred of self-doubt in my soul, so I was always saddened when I encountered individuals who were plagued with feelings of inadequacy or depression. I wanted to wave a magic wand to take away any unhappiness that clung to them.

This desire to encourage others to find their way out of depression or self-doubt often put me in the position of encouraging my women friends to recognize their unique qualities and cultivate feelings of self-worth. This was a role I felt quite comfortable with, though it frustrated me when I couldn't simply transfer my ebullience to others. It seemed to me so natural and obvious to look at life with self-love, enthusiasm, and joy. After graduation from college, I accepted a position in the pharmaceutical industry, traveling throughout the world. In that position, I had even more opportunities to work with and encourage women to love and appreciate themselves. My desire to encourage women to follow their dreams and live up to their full potential became even more fervent, and in this quest for the most meaningful language and methodology, I met Dr. Zannah Hackett. I believe that when the student is ready, the teacher will come, and that is precisely what happened. I knew without hesitation that The Knowledge of Y.O.U.® was exactly the methodology that would give me the tools to assist women in living up to their full potential. It is a precise and unique science that accelerates the process of self-discovery. My life has been deeply enriched with this knowledge, and it has been my pleasure and honor to pass it on. It is a gift.

The Answer

David J. Hackett
CEO, Y.O.U. Consulting Group
Master Life Coach and Relationship Expert

As CEO and co-founder of the Y.O.U. Consulting Group, I get to see and experience personal transformation on a daily basis. It first started over ten years ago, when I met my wife, partner, and the most important person in my life, Dr. Zannah Hackett. I had no idea at the time that our lives would unfold into a menu of service to our fellow men and women, but there was an instantaneous "knowing" or magnetic attraction that I felt for her when my eyes first gazed upon her angelic glow back on January 4, 1999.

This is not a love story, and I'm not going to get all "mushy" here, but there is a scientific explanation as to why two people are attracted to one another that goes beyond sheer physicality. Those who can "see" or who have training in the use of The Ultimate Life Tool® and The Knowledge of Y.O.U.® possess the unique ability to instantly know and "see" the people they are looking at, using its multi-dimensional methodology of five specific parts that are based on natural law and grounded in science.

Sounds kinda' "trippy," huh? Well, it's not. It's really one of the most important and cutting-edge breakthroughs in human assessment technology today—and put in the hands and minds of responsible leaders, trainers, psychologists, and others who

are in the business of helping others maximize their potential—
it is truly a gift to this lifetime.

The Ultimate Life Tool® is The Answer® to some of the most
common questions men and women ask themselves in this
lifetime: *Who am I? Why do I do the things I do? What should
I do with my life? Why do I like her/him?* And the list goes on
and on.

That day Zannah and I met, she could "see" me, all my
strengths and all my potential weaknesses. All I could *see* was
a beautiful redhead. They say in the world of relationships, "you
can only attract what you are," and I was clearly not feeling up
to the level of unconditional love she was expressing to me
when we first met. I immediately started referring to her as "the
Angel Goddess of Divine Love."

I had never met a woman who loved everyone unconditionally.
In fact, most of the women in my life came with *huge* expectations,
anger, resentment, and baggage so large it should have been
shipped via FedEx! You see, I was already a divorced father in
recovery who was certain that marriage, like any other story,
had a beginning, a middle, and an end! And I was certain that
I would never partake in that "end drama" again. I saw no point
in it. The thought of failing again was too devastating (not to
mention expensive), so during our courtship, I informed Zannah
that marriage for me was *absolutely out of the question.* This
information didn't bother her at all; she didn't even flinch!

I thought to myself, *How is that possible that a woman who
has been just told that I will never marry her did not get upset
or bolt out the nearest door?* Maybe she knew something I
didn't? Maybe she knew a lot that I didn't? Maybe, just maybe,
she possessed some hidden knowledge of what I needed in

the context of a relationship that I had no idea even existed? She could "see" me.

Beyond "seeing" me, she knew how to "feed" me. She knew what made me "thrive" instead of just "survive" in a relationship. What important and invaluable information to have! This is something that could, in fact, transform the world into a more understanding and loving place. A place where we all had the ability to "see" others as the perfection of the divine creations we all are.

The Knowledge of Y.O.U.® is just that: an objective body of knowledge enabling human beings to "see" one another using the natural laws that govern this physical existence: gravity, electromagnetism, and nuclear forces.

These are the things Zannah could see, honor, and measure in me. This is what gave her a unique insight as to what kind of "vehicle" I am. We have now been married almost ten years, and our relationship has only gotten better and better each year. Better communication, deeper trust, and a ton of fun (and challenging times and situations) have only made our bond stronger and our relationship better; the only difference this time around is that we have the tools to understand and honor each other using this cutting-edge technology.

Men are not usually in the business of managing love relationships. That is usually up to the woman. Women are designed to do this; it's in their nature. In fact, usually when a relationship fails, it's the woman's fault. Great news for us men, right? Now, by no means am I saying that men should not take responsibility for their part in making any relationship successful; however when it comes down to it, women say when the relationship is "on" and also when it's over. They are also the one in the relationship with the ability to "expand" and "contract" and "move" within the context of the bond.

The Knowledge of Y.O.U.® explains how and why this works, and in fact, how the dynamics of any relationship works. After all, isn't life all about relationships? I know mine is. Our company, the Y.O.U. Consulting Group, is committed to creating perfect relationships in business, home and life through the use of The Knowledge of Y.O.U.® and The Ultimate Life Tool®.

In addition to using The Ultimate Life Tool® and The Knowledge of Y.O.U.® as the first tools of choice when assisting couples in healing and understanding each other in the context of their relationships, I have also used the Knowledge and the Tool to assist many people in any twelve-step recovery program in understanding what the root cause of their addiction is and how they can use the knowledge to successfully get sober and stay sober using their new understanding of themselves.

Over the last ten years, Dr. Zannah and I have had the wonderful opportunity to not only experience a beautiful, loving, wonderful, fun, and empowering relationship, we have had the honor to coach and mentor others who value relationships on their journey by implementing The Knowledge of Y.O.U.® through various treatment strategies that have allowed relationships of all kinds to experience the true nature of life itself and ultimately unconditional love.

I welcome you to Take The Ultimate Life Tool® and change your perspective on life forever.

Perfection

Sondra Santos LaBrie
YCG Certified Practitioner

Growing up, I struggled with constantly trying to be someone I was not. I knew I was different, unique, and unlike anybody else out there. Despite that knowledge, I was constantly bouncing in and out of social groups, reinventing myself to try and fit in.

In college, I chose to study psychology, mostly because I was curious about people, myself especially. I took classes on public speaking, professional writing, communication, debate, drama, poetry, and music—none of which applied to my major or added credits toward my degree. I took them because I wanted desperately to find the path that was meant for me.

I ended up learning more about myself than I ever imagined. I confirmed and began to grow comfortable with the fact that I *am* different. I *am* unique. I *am* unlike anybody else out there. That is true for each and every one of us.

The Ultimate Life Tool® was introduced to me at a time when I was, once again, trying to reinvent myself. In less than ten years, I had experienced so many life-changing events (miscarriage, a cross-country move, marriage, a new career, childbirth, and divorce) that some might say that I survived my midlife crisis already, although I realize that the "Interval" is still around the corner.

The personality tests, assessments, and surveys that I studied in college intrigued me but never quite answered the questions I had or provided any solid solutions. When Dr. Zannah Hackett first shared the story with me of *The Cactus and the Willow Tree,* I finally "got" it. I realized what I had been missing all along and I was instantly hooked.

Since becoming a practitioner, I have used The Knowledge of Y.O.U.® in both my personal and professional life. I have seen the amazing results of being able to recognize, understand, and validate those around me, including family and friends, and even clients and potential business partners.

As a certified parent educator and parent coach, I am able to use The Ultimate Life Tool® to help parents see their children, parents, siblings, or co-parent, and provide them with real solutions instead of advice.

We joke with one another all the time about our *imperfections.* At the same time, we acknowledge that babies come into this world as perfect little beings. *So what happens? What or when is that defining moment when we start to become less than perfect?*

With the knowledge, I have been able to help both children and adults embrace their individuality, acknowledge their strengths and accept their weaknesses, becoming more forgiving of themselves and more understanding of others.

Investing in the health and well-being of those in your family is something that we all strive for in this lifetime. We continually seek or create new tools, methods, and practices that might help us find the key to successful relationships.

I truly believe that The Knowledge of Y.O.U.® holds that key, not only because of the results I have seen, but also because of the awareness that I have experienced, both firsthand and what I have witnessed in others.

The energy, time, and effort put into the creation of The Ultimate Life Tool®— and this book—is only the beginning. You're reading this because you are on the right path, one that is meant for you alone. You have surrounded yourself with loving and supportive individuals and have made choices in your life that have led you to this new technology.

Continue to do what you're doing. The Knowledge of Y.O.U.® is yours to discover and will provide you with so much insight into why and how we do things or react certain ways that the awareness that it brings is invaluable.

I am continually amazed and inspired by the dynamic and diverse group of individuals who are a part of the Y.O.U. Consulting Group. They have helped so many people discover the natural path that was created for them, and I am truly grateful to belong to this wonderful organization.

<u>TAKE THREE</u>

Dave Scahill
YCG Certified Practitioner

I have been blessed in my life in many ways. I first met my wife Denise twenty-nine years ago, when she was as senior in high school . As of September 2009, we have been married for twenty-five years!

Marriage has been a blessing for me. It has offered me stability, where as a kid I moved a lot. In fact, I went to eight schools in twelve years. Even though I was born in the Midwest, my first memories were of Southern California, where I lived when I was between four and eight years of age. Two days after marrying Denise in Chicago, we moved to San Diego—and I have never looked back. I believe this manifested in part as a result of my appreciation for the works of Napoleon Hill. As a result, I positively *believed* us back to California.

Since that time, we have been blessed with two wonderful boys who have now become young men: Shawn is twenty and Patrick is seventeen. We have dedicated ourselves to being there for them and raising them to the best of our ability. It has been the best part of our lives so far. They are a joy to be with, and we are all living in harmony together.

I have also been blessed to have a career that has provided fulfillment in my life in every way. We were able to afford for

Denise to stay home with our boys, and we have the home, the cars, and other resources of our dreams. I have developed long-term relationships with many of my customers and co-workers. This fulfills my natural need to connect with people. I have the opportunity to present myself and my company's deliverables every week, fulfilling my need to be in front of people. But most importantly, I have the opportunity and privilege in helping people fulfill their needs and wants. This includes setting new goals for myself and the future that lies ahead, and this takes passion. Some of the things I embrace most are loving my family and being loved by them, watching children at play, mentoring others to success, teaching, creating excitement for new ideas, executing plans into action, and boating, baseball, and barbecues with friends.

My first experience with personal development came on a road trip just before Denise and I became engaged. We were unsure if we wanted to stay together and nurture our relationship and then get married or go our separate ways as friends. We drove for two days in silence, talking, yelling, crying, more silence, talking, yelling, crying, more silence, and then we found the great Napoleon Hill's final book titled *Grow Rich with Peace of Mind.* His words brought Denise and me to a new level of thinking and understanding of each other's desires, goals, and needs for a successful and fulfilling life. That book changed our lives and helped us to realize our dreams. I became a student of self-realization and positive mental attitude. I consistently work on implementing what I learn.

Then one day, after twenty-three years of happily working for the same company, I decided to start looking to make a change. I chose to go to a random meeting of executives in transition, where the keynote speaker was David Hackett, the CEO of the Y.O.U. Consulting Group. I was inspired to know more about YCG and called David to learn more about the Knowledge of Y.O.U.® David asked me to take the "Ultimate Life Tool"® test and come and meet with him and Dr. Zannah.

After spending one afternoon with the Hacketts, I decided to learn as much as I could about myself and those closest to me. The Knowledge of Y.O.U.® is a very powerful tool that helps you realize what and who you really are and why we do the things we do naturally. Knowing yourself and loving yourself, just the way you are is easier said than done, but having the Knowledge of Y.O.U.® helps you *see* yourself and those you love most. We are all very special and unique, and honoring ourselves by accepting yourself and others can bring amazing results.

Creating perfect relationships is truly possible with the "Ultimate Life Tool" and the Knowledge of Y.O.U.® and my mission for the next phase of my life is to work toward building a team of consultants worldwide who can help bring joy, happiness, and fulfillment to all who join us on our journey of self-mastery.

ENERGY and Y.O.U.

Paula Shaw

CADC, DCEP

YCG Certified Practitioner

As a student of quantum physics and one of the pioneers in the field of energy psychology, I was well aware that "everything is energy." I have attended countless conferences and read volumes of literature that had me well informed that everything in the universe is made up of, and formed by, electromagnetic energy. I knew that I (and everything else in creation) am simply a conglomeration of energy vibrating at different frequencies. Energy shapes me, motivates me, breathes through me, and attracts to me other vibrating frequencies of energy.

I had expertise in shifting or neutralizing frequencies when they became problematic. Consequently, I developed a system in the field of energy psychology referred to as conscious healing and re-patterning therapy, which I shared with audiences in the United States and Europe.

And yet, in spite of this experience and my belief in the rapid healing power of energy psychology techniques (and while I totally believe this is the psychology of the future) I had yet to find a way that it helped me deal with the challenging task of accepting myself just as I am. In fact, being well versed in the powerful tools of this field, I had an even more difficult time avoiding the temptation to keep experimenting with using them in the never-ending attempt to perfect myself.

Like so many people, I had grown up believing that self-love was selfish and self-acceptance was just an unwillingness to look at the problem areas that needed changing. I was gung ho to find my blocks and limitations and clear them, so I could have that perfect life and that perfect me. To have just accepted who I am and what I am was quite honestly unacceptable. That would mean that my ongoing self-improvement campaign was now without a focus or a goal. What would I do if that happened? What would I feel chagrined or embarrassed about? Where would I find myself lacking? Where would I target the reading of the next self-help book?

Enter ... The Knowledge of Y.O.U.® I met Dr. Zannah Hackett because her husband David, with whom I was taking a class, had a feeling that we would hit it off and should meet. Suffice it to say he was more than right. Not only did we love each other, she changed my life in a two-hour meeting.

Dr. Zannah proceeded to tell me all these fascinating things about why our physicality has valid impact on what you are and what you need to experience to be energetically fed. She talked to me about what is needed in our environment in order to be comfortable. She shared about what a woman needs to do to keep a man happy in a relationship. But where she really hooked me in was when she said that the knowledge is grounded in science and founded in the laws of nature, particularly focusing on gravity, electromagnetism, and nuclear force. She was talking about energy. This was a language I understood.

I was starting to light up at the concepts being presented to me. After being invited to "Take the Test", I found that one simple test drive opens up a world you didn't know existed and nothing is ever the same again. A new kind of thinking emerges and you realize that maybe the "model" you arrived as is perfect just the way it is.

This is revolutionary thinking, because what we more commonly do is agonize, criticize, and lament over what we are and are not. You know the experience: It's like we arrive as, say, an SUV and we spend our lives lamenting that we aren't a Porsche. We are big and roomy and lofty, and we are dying to be sleek and fast and sexy. So instead of loving what we are and appreciating the benefits of it, we spend our lives trying to modify the basic design to look like something else.

So, okay, you're wondering how this knowledge helped me with my inability to accept myself. Well, it helped me see very clearly that I arrived on the planet as the model that I am, and like it or not, there is very little I can do to change that basic model, especially not through criticism and judgment. I am what I am, and I realized that a wise person just accepts that, loves it, and works with it, rather than continuing to expend volumes of energy in disapproval, judgment, and desire for change. I'm not just talking about the physical package. It's equally rare that we accept the way we think, behave, and emote. We are always judging our thoughts and behaviors. And if you are like me, you are always trying to change and improve them. The idea of "embracing my weaknesses" never crossed my mind in any serious way. And, of course, you can bet that if you can't accept flaws in yourself, you have a very difficult time accepting them in others.

What this knowledge has done for me is increase my tolerance and love for myself and for all the other people in my life. Now when I hear someone say, "It's not about you; it's just Erin being Erin," I get it. I see my friends, family, and clients in a whole new way. I get why they do what they do without being baffled or critical. This knowledge puts love on a whole new level and has greatly helped me in my relationship counseling and my work with grieving people. I don't have to put on my "professional hat" to understand and accept my clients. I just do, because I see that they are all going down the road of life as the SUV, Porsche, Jeep, or Hummer that they are. The Porsche wants to go fast and look good. The SUV feels that he's king of the road, and the Jeep wants adventure. There is nothing to criticize now; it all makes sense and it's all fun. What a difference a "test drive" can make. Thank you, Dr. Zannah and The Knowledge of Y.O.U.®

In Search of Thyself

Annie Hodkgins
HR Training Specialist
YCG Certified Practitioner

I'm not sure when I first began on my search, but it seems I have always been driven to understand myself and others. Who knows how many self-help books I've read? The answer is easily hundreds in the past three decades. I've given away as many as still populate my shelves and boxes, and then some. I've spent thousands of hours and thousands of dollars in seminars and workshops as well. I shared my search with friends and family and wanted to help others who were seeking this same understanding. I became certified in a number of personal assessment tools that I used successfully for nearly two decades in my personal life and in my personal consulting business, as a trainer and facilitator. I worked with private clients and business owners. I was a contract trainer working on behalf of the Chrysler Corporation and for Ford Motor Company. I worked with thousands of people. I loved using these tools, such as DISC, four factor model, and TICS values profiles as a means to open people up while team-building or implementing culture changes in organizations.

However, prior to gaining access to The Knowledge of Y.O.U.®, there seemed to be something missing. I was always working to supplement the limitations of those behavioral models, as wonderful and helpful as they were. I love the experience of self-discovery and those experiences have absolutely helped me along my way providing insight, as mostly an intellectual function. My own life experience and love for people and the kind of vehicle I am (as we practitioners of The Knowledge of Y.O.U.® say) fosters the compassion for our human condition. A student of life is who I am, and will likely always be.

While I had learned much, I had not yet entered a state of a new seeking, a new quest. The old information seemed to be not so relevant, somewhat superficial. I had become a bit jaded and cynical; I was looking for a deeper understanding. Why was I finding myself doing the things I was doing? Why did I give up a career of almost thirty years to pursue an entirely new direction? Why did it take me eight years to divorce my husband of thirty-four years? Why was I attracted to certain people, and why did I seem to *need* to dance like I needed to breathe?

And then, a dear friendship with my best friend, Zannah, that had remained intact since fourth grade, resurfaced after some time being out of touch. While we came together over the passing of her father—the man who used to make lunch for us and listen to our girlish play—she was eager to tell me of her latest work. She was so excited to share it with me, and without having any understanding of it, I tried to stack it up next to my frame of reference. I complained to her about the limitations of behavioral models I had worked with and some of the reasons I no longer used them. I had an innate mistrust of yet another model. She would agree with my evaluations and tell me a bit more about the "knowledge." My previous work with different self-assessment tools could not stand up to Zannah's new work. All my comparisons limited it and gave me no insight other than to ultimately know that it was beyond comparison. Eventually, I took the survey and got my results back. It took at least another two years before I could begin to appreciate the depth and value of the information she was offering. By then, I was willing, though still a bit guarded about "another survey." I found myself in The Knowledge of Y.O.U.® Practitioner I Training.

Slowly I began to comprehend the nature of this knowledge. I wondered if I would ever *"get it."* As I listened to Zannah, I began to "see." It was amazing and wonderful, and I was in awe! Truly in awe. It has been an absolute pleasure and a newfound dimension and capacity unleashed in my life for compassion, understanding, and acceptance for our individual differences.

One of my most delightful discoveries occurred after finishing my Practitioner II training. After arriving home in Rio Verde, I attended my niece Jackie's college graduation at Arizona State University. I have loved this darling girl in a way that I find impossible to explain or describe since she was born. I was so pleased that I could attend. My brother, Jackie's father Greg, and Jackie's mother Kristen, her brother Jimmy, and her fiancé Jacob and his mother and father, and Jackie's grandparents were all there.

We somehow found ourselves with an almost unobstructed view of Jackie, who was in the front row! As I was taking pictures with my Pentax, I was stunned to "see" my niece for the first time, as we practitioners say. I was covered in goose bumps to realize the answers to some of my questions about her, things I'd always wanted to understand about her behavior, but I seriously had no clue. All my experience and knowledge could not provide the answers.

When I "saw" her through this body of knowledge—The Knowledge of Y.O.U.® interestingly enough—I also realized that we had these traits in common. Up to the point at which I received my training, I didn't see it in myself—or in Jackie. It was a moment of "aha!" and amazement for me and an even deeper feeling of love and connection for my niece and greater clarity for understanding myself.

What was it I saw? I saw the reasons for her ability to write and communicate, use her artistic talents, and to be a visionary. I saw and understood her behavior at family gatherings that seemed to have her always melting into the background. I understood her true strength of humility. Jackie demonstrated this in a unique way at her graduation. She failed to mention to anyone that she was graduating *summa cum laude*. This is so like Jackie. I will never forget this precious moment.

The possibility for each one who wants to have this knowledge would be a huge gift to mankind. Or maybe just for you. It was my childhood friend, Zannah's gift to me.

A Reverence for Life

Monica Lucas-Magnusson
Holistic Health Practitioner
YCG Certified Practitioner

From a young age I knew that life was something to be cherished. Perhaps it was how I grew up that helped to form that belief, but I really feel that it was just how I showed up. The choices I made in my own personal life were always based on the outcome and what I could contribute to the planet; that's a deep thought for a kid, but to me it was quite natural. It was also quite natural when I grew up and the beckoning question from my elders was "What are you going to do with your life?" For me, the answer was "Help heal the planet" and so my journey began.

After I graduated from school, I found myself in a career in the medical industry, working for a large corporate health maintenance organization. It was there that I learned the "business" of health care. After thirteen years of that experience, I retired so that I could follow my real passion which was teaching people to listen and know themselves so they could be healthy.

It was from my own health challenge that I understood that humans are not just one-dimensional and that when a disease manifests physically, it is also related to the mental and emotional body. Since education has always been a focus in my life, I went back to school to become a holistic health practitioner. As I completed that credential, I also became a licensed hypnotherapist, master NLP practitioner, registered yoga instructor, and certified professional co-active coach. I thought my toolbox was filled with all that I needed to successfully work with a person and help them to identify and heal their bodies and their life. As a holistic practitioner and owner of Spa Mode, a "Healthy Lifestyle Boutique and Day Spa," I immediately saw how The Ultimate Life Tool® technology could benefit my clients. It was, as I call it, the "icing on the cake" and it made everything else I knew make sense. It provided a deeper level of understanding and it worked. My clients were getting the results they wanted!

The Knowledge of Y.O.U.® to me really is The Ultimate Life Tool® technology, and I have found it to be invaluable to my practice and to me personally, and here is why: this knowledge is scientific and is based in natural law. Our planet is governed by these laws and so are we, yet we weren't taught to see ourselves as nature sees itself. I learned that when we look at a tree, we know what kind of tree it is. We also know what kind of environment it is suited for. But when we look at humans, we don't use the same thought process; we think it's more complicated. Nature is intricate but not complicated, and so are we. It is that intricacy that makes life itself so special; it is the intricacies that make everything relate. Simply put, nature is about relationships.

I spent a good part of my twenties and most of my thirties trying to "see" myself and relate to who I was. As a kid, I intuitively knew what was authentic to my nature but unfortunately, I stopped listening to nature. I began to listen to those who I thought knew better. So the idiosyncrasies that did not fit into the box of those around me became harsh judgments and negative beliefs. However, it was when I learned *what I was,* I began to embrace all *that I am.* From this knowledge, I realized as an adult that how I showed up in this life was indeed to be one that facilitates healing, and I became aware that the authentic qualities given me empowered me. What I believed to be wrong about me no longer mattered because it was all right and that created a special relationship with me; it also allowed me to create stronger relationships with those I care about. From all perspectives, this knowledge applied in my relationships, marriage, family, friends, colleagues, and clients.

As a certified practitioner in The Knowledge of Y.O.U.® and The Ultimate Life Tool® Technology, I am passionate about educating both youth and adults alike to see themselves in nature's way, support a healthy lifestyle, and to live optimally. It is my mission still to bring healing to the planet and it is that responsibility that serves my deepest driving desires, because that's just who I am.

Happily Ever After

Janice Ross

MS Psychology, Jbird Distribution

I am writing this on the day of my first anniversary of my marriage to the love of my life. I do not know if I would be having this glorious anniversary without understanding the knowledge behind the Ultimate Life Tool®

Childhood was tough for me. My father passed away from a sudden heart attack when I was eight. Life was never the same or even close to normal. My mother passed away from breast and bone cancer four years later. I always felt different because I was the one with no parents. I felt that I was "less than." And sadly, that is how I felt for most of my life.

I made a promise to myself when I was young: I would never be fat and I would never be poor. My parents were overweight, and in my childish mind, I thought that contributed to their early deaths. I was determined to not be left behind because I had no parents. I would just have to work harder to make it and never be poor.

Consequently, I have worked my whole life to accomplish these objectives. I still work very hard and exercise most days. With this being said, my personal life was a *mess*. I could never figure out why or what everyone else knows. There was no one to teach me.

Meeting Zannah Hackett was one of the most significant events in my life. It was Christmas Eve 1997, and she was my great gift. We have been close friends ever since, even though we both get busy in life. We go weeks or months without talking and we still know we are there for each other. Prior to meeting her, I bought and read every self-help book available. I couldn't figure out what was wrong. I had a million questions roaming around in my head. What kind of being am I? What is my strength? What is my weakness? Why does it feel like everyone is walking down a solid path and I am always on an unstable slippery slope? How did I end up single for seventeen years? What am I doing wrong?

Then I learned simple lessons in the Knowledge that were always right in front of my face and I just did not know them. The most important lesson was to recognize myself.

Then I learned about tolerance and refinement. Once my eyes were open, I could see the examples all around me. There is an objective frame of reference regarding the laws of refinement. Now I could see my own level of refinement and know what I could accept and what I could never achieve. It taught me my comfort zone. When a person is put into a level too far from their own, it causes one to feel discomfort, even though we may not be aware of why we are feeling out of sync. I am now in my perfect zone. This lesson was the easiest for me.

Over the course of time, I became aware of my personal style. This was great because now I also could recognize the type of man who would be my maximum attraction. Before this, I had been searching for someone "like" me. That doesn't always work. We need to *complement* each other. And today,

I am now surrounded by a love greater than anything I could have ever imagined or hoped for. I never knew or remembered what true unconditional love felt like until now.

Then there are the laws. The laws are as clear as the law of gravity. The most important law to me is the law of non-resistance. It took some great adjustment in my way of thinking and acting for me to internalize this law. I used to be the rock instead of the water. This law freed me from a lot of emotional turmoil.

Once I got some perspective on myself, I also got perspective on those around me. I could see the nature of people and what motivated them. I could see the refinement levels in my children, friends, and co-workers. The knowledge helped me with all of my relationships. I learned to be more receptive to others' perspectives and ways of life. I especially recognize this in my children, who are all very different. I no longer expect everyone to do it my way.

It seems that every day the Knowledge of Y.O.U. is with me. It has surrounded my life. As I go through the day, I think of things in terms of what I learned.

As I meet new people, I can recognize what they are. I can see their refinement and I immediately know something more about that person before I even speak to them. I have a natural perspective. I know what to expect and what not to expect. I think in terms of the laws, too. I know about the law of three and the law of seven and how life just fits into these laws. I know there is always so much more for me to learn in the *Knowledge*. I am so thankful that Zannah and David made this knowledge available. For everyone who is educated in the Knowledge of Y.O.U., the benefit is theirs—but it extends to all who surround that person's life including friends, family, and business associates.

This *Knowledge* is life-changing for me. Think about how wonderful our planet would be if everyone had these simple tools. I am most grateful to Zannah for all of the hours, patience, and perseverance she put into me to change my life. I am now enjoying the fruits of our labor.

Appendix

William Bradstreet Stewart
Sacred Science Institute

Throughout history, mankind has searched for answers to the fundamental questions of who he is, why he is here, and where he is supposed to be going. Yet the answers to these essential questions seem to elude all but the most philosophical of beings, and even those who seem to have grasped the answers to these questions often seem to be in conflict with one another. Now, in an age of ever-increasing resources of information, the true answers to these questions have become even more difficult to ascertain, owing to the unquestioned dogmas and ulterior motives of the groups or individuals who purport to know "The Truth." Simple truths are made overly complex and impenetrable, while superficial insights are spun into complex and misleading realities that titillate the lower nature in the name of the higher. How does one navigate this labyrinth of complexity and misinformation in a way that is both meaningful to one's life and fulfilling to one's soul?

The Knowledge of Y.O.U.® provides an answer to these fundamental questions, by looking throughout history to the most reliable and consistent sources of wisdom, provided by the deepest and most respected thinkers and spiritual teachers throughout the ages. It develops a means of showing an individual his true authenticity, leading to a more authentic lifestyle, with a greater sense of fulfillment, in contradistinction to the disappointment so common today in the man who has no understanding of himself. This system of knowledge is often referred to as the perennial philosophy, a tradition of wisdom discovered in all cultures, regardless of their place in history, their social context, or geographical location. The essential premise of this tradition is that knowledge is inherent in the structure of human consciousness, and that deep reflection, experience, and insight inherently lead to the same ultimate conclusions. As human beings, we all possess the same essential hardware and software that make up our nature. Likewise, we all experience the same fundamental characteristics of our environment: the need for food, clothing, shelter, and relationships both personal and social, though tempered by varied sociological, economic, political, and religious contexts.

The tradition of perennial philosophy seeks that which is the same within the context of that which appears to be different, and discovers that in the face of the ever-changing world, the ultimate spiritual conclusions and personal meanings for human existence remain constant. The reason that there is an inherent consistency in the nature of these answers is that the underlying architecture of reality is based upon fundamental principles or templates, called archetypes. Archetypes are universal patterns upon which everything is modeled, from physical reality, to emotional response, to conceptual patterns. In the same manner that there are laws that govern the nature of physical reality (as explored by physics, biology, chemistry, and cosmology), there are similar laws that govern the function of each level of our being. Further, there is a correspondence between the laws within each system, allowing for one to draw analogies between seemingly different systems, by applying

206

laws understood in one, for the development of insight into another that is not understood.

An example of such an analogy is the use of terms developed through computer science to explain human brain function. Concepts such as our brains being a form of biological hardware (while our various thinking process and programming provide the operating system and software) were unimaginable only fifty years ago, before the advent of the computer era. Yet, at the same time that computer models have provided templates for conceptualizing the functioning of the human brain, advances in neurological science have provided models that have been developed into new kinds of computer programming, such as neural nets and the like. This process demonstrates how archetypal templates have a universal essence that is applicable, through the law of analogy, to seemingly varied fields of knowledge and application.

These ancient traditions characterized by the perennial philosophy similarly recognized the value of these archetypal patterns and learned to seek these templates, existing within what Plato called—more than two millennia ago—the *realm of ideas.* In Plato's philosophy, there was an abstract universal realm characterized by these idea templates, or archetypes, which formed the conceptual and structural basis for everything in the manifested universe. By understanding the nature and function of these ideas, one could understand the essence of anything. Similarly, in the Yogacara and Hua Yen schools of Buddhism, there is a concept called the *alyavijnana* (or, the storehouse consciousness), in which are contained the essential "seeds" of thought, which when provided with energy, produce everything existent in the manifest world (physical, mental, or otherwise). These concepts, though from different cultures and different times, were developed along similar lines of thought, and were discovered through the cognitive and introspective processes of the mind. It is because the hardware and software of the human system are built according to consistent structures that different, unassociated systems of knowledge produce the same fundamental insights and understandings.

Similarly, it has been noted that modern physics, with its recent discovery of such complex theories as quantum mechanics and relativity, has developed strikingly similar perspectives to ancient traditions such as the Vedantic, Taoist, and Buddhist theories of consciousness. Yet, modern scientists are not studying the structure and function of the mind and consciousness in the way that these ancient mystic traditions were, through introspection and spiritual practice. They are experimenting within the nature of the physical universe, from the infinitesimally small world of high-energy particle physics, to the infinitesimally vast world of cosmological astrophysics. How could these seemingly disparate fields of study produce such similar perspectives and conclusions if there were not a directly correlative structure underlying everything from physical reality to human consciousness?

Similar examples of such correlations between archetypal principles derived from seemingly different fields of knowledge permeate the history of mankind, from the most ancient civilizations of which we have historical record, from Egypt, India, China, Mesoamerica, and Sumer, to the remnants of mysterious, prehistoric cultures such as Atlantis, Lemuria, and other lost ancient civilizations, the remains of which are ever resurfacing through new archaeological research. These traditions have continued to propagate throughout history, right down to modern times, through advanced cultures such as the Greeks (represented by Plato and Pythagora), the early Muslims, (represented in their architectural and scientific traditions), the Mayans (represented by their vast astronomical and calendrical wisdom), as well as, in the face of social persecution, through more secret societies, like the Gnostics, the Alchemists, the Freemasons, and the Rosicrucians.

With the advent of the enlightenment and the scientific revolution, these traditions began to take new modern forms: alchemy developed into chemistry, astrology led to modern astronomy, esoteric cosmology morphed into modern physics, and mysticism became cloaked in philosophy and later psychology. The essential principles and elements can still be distinguished by looking to the underlying archetypal forms upon which each of these new sciences is based.

The modern forefather of the tradition presented in this book was a mystic/philosopher/scientist named G.I. Gurdjieff, who founded a school called the Fourth Way. Around the turn of the twentieth century, Gurdjieff, as a youth from the Caucasus Mountains of southern Russia, was deeply driven by a quest for the knowledge of man and the universe. He felt that there was a lost way of living which—if discovered—would provide man with a more meaningful and fulfilling existence. He formed a band of like-minded companions, called the Seekers of Truth, and together they traveled the world, seeking out lost traditions of knowledge, while simultaneously exploring the latest developments in modern science and psychology. They discovered that many of these ancient traditions possessed a better understanding of the problems confronting man than most modern traditions did, and they worked to integrate these two strains of thought into a more complete and applicable system of science and living. This tradition was passed down through a number of branches of the Fourth Way school, and provided the initial inspiration for The Knowledge of Y.O.U.®

In conjoining these ancient traditions of perennial philosophy with the new insights of modern science, a more complete system of philosophy and living was developed using these archetypes to provide a system of understanding one's true nature, by giving one an objective evaluation of the underlying elements of the individual psyche. These archetypes are often described in symbolic form or through numerical templates.

An excellent example of such symbology is the four elements: earth, air, fire, and water. These terms did not originally refer to the actual substances themselves, but to the principles that they represented: solid, gaseous, hot, and wet, and were interpreted more along the lines of specific qualities of energy or substance. In more modern terms, they could be considered similar to field forces or universal laws, and it is not a coincidence that in modern physics there are four fundamental forces: gravity, electromagnetism, and strong and weak nuclear forces. Carl Jung, father of modern depth psychology, developed a system of psychological typing based upon four temperaments: sanguine, melancholic, choleric, and phlegmatic, which directly correlate to these four elements, and can be traced back as far as five thousand years through ancient Greece and Egypt to

Mesopotamia. These temperaments have been incorporated into popular modern personality assessments, such as the Meyers-Briggs assessment, which has renamed them artisan, guardian, idealist, and rationalist. Even modern genetics research had discovered that there are only four fundamental amino acids that form the DNA, creating the template for all biological structure.

Another common symbolic numerical template is based upon the number seven. There are seven colors in the rainbow, seven tones to the musical scale, seven planets in the ancient solar system, and seven energy centers (or chakras) with their correlative glands in the endocrine system. The Knowledge of Y.O.U.® uses the template of the ancient planetary system as its symbolic format for describing the essential body types and correlative psychological components. This is not to be confused with some form of astrology, though the qualitative elements symbolically given to the planets possess similar attributes. These are universal archetypal templates, formative ordering processes, which are applicable throughout nature. As one begins to understand the relationships of this qualitative symbology, one will begin to see new levels of order and correspondence throughout everything in nature. The medieval alchemists called this process of seeing the correlations throughout the universe, "reading the book of nature." This book will help you to do the same.

In closing, we must ask ourselves the question, "Am I living and fulfilling my greatest potential?" If we do not answer this question with a resounding *yes,* then we must begin to ask, "Why am I not?" For only in knowing the right question is there a chance of finding the right answer. Engraved in stone above the entrance to the Platonic Academy were two words: "Know Thyself." It is for this sole purpose that The Knowledge of Y.O.U.® and is being shared with you now, that you may live a life of true authenticity and fulfill your highest potential. And who does not desire that?

Suggested Reading & Websites

Reality, Spirituality and Modern Man, David Hawkins, MD, PhD, Axial Publishing Company, 2008

The Age of Spiritual Machines: When Computers Exceed Human Intelligence, Ray Kurzwell, Penguin Books, 1997

Power vs. Force The Hidden Determinants of Human Behavior, David Hawkins, MD, PhD, Hay House, 2002

The Eye of the I, David Hawkins, MD, PhD, Veritus Publishing, 2001

Subjectivity and Reality, David Hawkins, MD, PhD, Veritus Publishing, 2003

Truth and Falsehood, David Hawkins MD, PhD, Atlasbooks Distribution Service, 2005

The Eye of the Spirit, Ken Wilber, Shambala Publications, 2001

Integral Psychology, Ken Wilber, Shambala Publications, 2000

Minding the Body Mending the Mind, Joan Boreysenko PhD, Bantam Books, 1987

The Wisdom of Florence Scovel Shinn: Four Complete Books by Florence Scovel Shinn, Florence Scovel Shinn, Simon & Schuster, 1989 First edition 1925

The Psychology of Man's Possible Evolution P.D. Ouspensky, Harvest Books, 2001

Tertium Organum, P.D. Ouspensky, Vintage Books, 1950

Making a New World. Bennett, J. G. Gurdjieff, Harper and Row, 1976

A Brief History of Time, Stephen Hawking, Kindle Books, 1998

The Nature of Space and Time, Stephen Hawking and Roger Penrose, Princeton Science Library, 1996

Foundations of Mixed Methods Research: Integrating Quantitative and Qualitative Approaches in the Social and Behavioral Sciences, Dr. Charles B. Teddlie and Abbas Tashakkori, Sage Publications, Inc. 2003

Interview with Ken Wilber On Critics, Integral Institute, My Recent Writing, and Other Matters of Little Consequence: A Shambhala Online Interview with Ken Wilber

**On the Nature of a Post-Metaphysical Spirituality*: Response to Habermas and Weis,* Ken Wilber. Posted on 8/6/2001.

Interview with Ken Wilber An Online Interview with Shambhala regarding the publication of One Taste, Daily Reflections on Integral Spirituality

The Book of Nature *(http://physicsworld.com/cws/article/print/26529)* by Robert P. Crease, December 2006

Is There a Theory of Everything? Michio Kaku *(http://www.pbs.org/wnet/hawking/mysteries/html/kaku2-1.html)*

The Greatest Salesman in the World, Og Mandiono, Bantam, 1988

On Truth and Reality The Dynamic Unity of Reality *www.spaceandmotion.com*

Spiritual Economics, Eric Butterworth, Unity House, 2001

The Sacred Science Institute Dedicated to the Rediscovery and Application of Sacred Science in all fields of Knowledge, Technology and Evolution. www.sacredscience.com

THE ULTIMATE LIFE TOOL® Advanced Human Assessment Technology for a better mankind *www.theultimatelifetool.com*

THE Y.O.U. Institute® A 501c3 corporation providing affordable educational and counseling services to financially challenged families, individuals and entities using accredited cutting edge curriculum, technologies and services to better facilitate an understanding of human nature for purposes of creating healthy relationships in business, home and life. www.youinstitute.org

If you are interested in any of the following services,

please contact YCG Today:

Seminars, Webinars and Speaking Engagements

Certification for Professionals

Life Management 101

How a Child Learns

The Ultimate Love Life

Surviving Parenthood

Inviting Employee Excellence

Leadership Development

Raising a Special Needs Child

Private Consultations

By phone or on premises

To have Dr. Zannah Hackett or one of YCG's Certified Master Trainers appear live at your next event, send a request to info@theultimatelifetool.com**, or call 1-877-517-9384**

A 501c3 Non-profit organization dedicated

to helping individuals better understand themselves and others.

The Y.O.U. Institute uses The Ultimate Life Tool® technology and YCG certified professionals in addressing the following needs:

Couples Counseling

Families in Transition

Single Parenting

Teens in Crisis

Divorce Recovery

Career Discovery

Pre-marital Awareness

For full details, go to *www.youinstitute.org*

Or call 1-877-517-9384

The Author

Dr. Zannah Hackett is an educator, author, relationship technologist, and life advisor. She was born in La Jolla, California, grew up in Arizona, received degrees from Arizona State University and spent many years in the field of education, training and staff development. Among Zannah's many career pursuits, her role as Director of Health Services Development for Samaritan Hospitals exposed her to a growing need for outreach services in the community.

As a child, Zannah spent a great deal of time with her mother, Elizabeth Evans, at work. In 1958, Elizabeth was the first R.N. to supervise The Valley of the Sun School, a home for developmentally disabled children. Zannah played with these special children daily, recognizing them only as different and perfect. Her youth was often enriched by smiles and hugs given freely by dwarfs, down syndrome, hydrocephalic and mongoloid playmates. It was her perspective of "perfection" that gave her a view of life from a slightly more natural vantage point. As the years progressed Zannah would accomplish many things, travel the world and participate in think tanks with individuals that valued the evolution and exploration of the movement of man and his unwavering uniqueness. In 1998, she received her ministerial license from the ADL, The Alliance of Divine Love, an interfaith non-denominational ministry and in 2008 she completed her Doctorate. Her dissertation entitled " INTEGRAL PHYSICALITY AS IT INTERFACES WITH

SPIRITUAL INTEGRITY, HUMAN PERFORMANCE AND THE UNIQUE POLARIZED MATHEMATICS OF MAN REVEALING THE KNOWLEDGE OF Y.O.U. AND A NEW HOLISTIC LIFE SCIENCE TECHNOLOGY FOR MANKIND" served to launch the understanding that marks the beginning of a new era of human integration and self-awareness.

After fourteen years of diligent research and fortitude, Zannah holds fast to the notion that "GOD" does not make mistakes, MAN does. She believes that if man were to "SEE" himself through the eyes of Mother Nature and Father Time, he would better understand the gift of God...he is.

Giving mankind back his eyesight is her goal. She believes when you can "see" WHAT stands before you, rather than who, then and only then can you master yourself. Spirituality serves to dust off the daily pollution of this lifetime but understanding the laws that govern our Physicality while it concurrently intersects with our Spirituality is the only way self-mastery can be achieved. To date, great minds from all over the world come to her for clarity and a chance of catching a glimpse of reality as well as themselves.

Dr. Zannah and her devoted colleagues recently founded The Y.O.U. Institute, a non-profit entity, whose mission is to provide education, community outreach classes and advisement to those individuals and entities that cannot afford it otherwise. It is clear that her greatest gift to this lifetime is her dedicated team of certified educated professionals which include some of today's leading executive coaches, therapists, psychologists, educators, scientists, theologians and more. They take great pride in promoting and serving mankind by sharing their skill in delivering the "common sense" remembered through this cutting edge technology. Given the hundreds of hours they have invested in mastering the Knowledge and its technological application, Dr. Zannah knows they are the leading pioneers that will take it and The Y.O.U. Institute far beyond where it is today. As each day passes and new universal norms are exposed, it becomes clear that this work is her legacy. It changes lives, offers practical solutions to real physical challenges. If there is a human in the equation, a trained expert can offer an objective perspective and solid guidance as it relates to the client's personal uniqueness and their ongoing relationship with everything in life.

Zannah is equally grateful for her husband, David Hackett, a legendary world-class athlete, speaker and excellent recovery coach. She met him in 1999 after being single for 9 years. She used the Knowledge to recognize what was perfect for her in finding a mate and a relationship that would contribute to her own personal growth and fulfillment. Together they have four grown children and a grand-daughter. She thanks God everyday for her Advisory Board, her husband, and the continued commitment of Nanz Zekela, Lisa Nelson, Christine Hughes, Dr. Beth Wade, Niloo Tavangar, Hal Taylor, Nick Pearce, Dr. Ed Abeyta, Dr Charles Richards and Saundra Pelletier in seeing to it that this "return to reasonability" continues for the remainder of man as a species. Dr. Zannah moved to California permanently in 1988 and has resided in Encinitas for 21 years.

UNDERSTANDING MORE ...

In brief, The Ultimate Life Tool® technology distills motivational, behavioral and interest evaluation into a single assessment, which provides a multi-dimensional and comprehensive analysis. The knowledge is objective; meaning you don't have to give anything up to embrace and understand what motivates you and others. Current psychometric instruments have greater meaning when The Ultimate Life Tool® technology is used as a precursor. It provides a place for other test results to exist, adding more value and enhancing a greater understanding of human nature.

Unlike most other popular assessments, this instrument provides unique insights into underlying needs and motivations as they relate to physical law. Toxic situations and *dis*-ease are identified and explained when these needs are not met. Recognizing specific authentic needs and motivations and the consequences of these unmet needs gives the consultant, coach, practitioner, counselor and organizational development professional an effective way to improve personal and interpersonal workplace performance. This helps to reduce toxicity, conflict, and create a greater influx of intelligence overall. The outcome offers increased performance, increased revenue for the company and a deeper understanding of friends, co-workers, family and all others who touch our lives.

In brief, The Ultimate Life Tool® addresses five categories:

1. Traits - An individual's natural physical style they are born with giving us a unique insight into that persons' needs and motivations.

2. Motivation – What drives a person or motivates them to do the things they do and how these can get "Fed" or honored so they can accomplish their goals and rise to their full potential.

3. Boundaries - an individual's personal preferences and level of tolerance in others and environments.

4. Communication Style – Each individual's mode of how they learn, communicate and process information. Understanding our energy centers as they relate to communication is vital in reaching one's full potential.

5. Perception – Defines each person's Electromagnetic Potential. Whether they are Positive or Negative, (Both are good) it's just the individual's personal approach to finding what is "not working" or "what is working" first.

The Y.O.U. Ultimate Life Tool® Report

The Y.O.U. Ultimate Life Tool®, aka ULT, is always delivered online. Certified YCG Practitioner/Coaches thoroughly review reports in preparation for consultations. YCG's customers and licensees can access a variety of different reports and have the flexibility to combine reports specific to their specific needs. The Knowledge of Y.O.U. was introduced in 2005 and gives executive coaches, healthcare providers and human resource professionals a powerful tool based on the Knowledge of Y.O.U. and The Ultimate Life Tool® technology. Coursework is accredited by the California State Board of Behavioral Sciences and The California Board of Registered Nursing. Upon completing the online test, clients receive a 7 to 10 page report , often referred to as an "operating manual". The written results serve to define and recommend ways in which to maximize their perception, intelligence, tolerance, energy pool, strengths and the act of making conscious choices.

A Wide Range of Applications

As an advanced cutting edge nature-based scientific instrumentation for measuring human behavior and occupational strengths, The Ultimate Life Tool® provides a wide range of applications including:

Pre-Employment	Conflict Management
Individual Development	Stress Management
Team Building	Culture Management
Team Development	Mergers and Acquisitions
Career Guidance	Workplace Diversity
Career Management	Succession Planning
Career Transition	Crisis Management
Coaching	Retirement Planning
Executive Coaching	Pre & Post Marital Coaching
Leadership Development	Recovery Advisement
Education & the Classroom	Healthcare
Alternative Healing	Talent Management

INDEX

CPSIA information can be obtained at www.ICGtesting.com
Printed in the USA
LVOW06s0821051013

355509LV00002B/88/P